FEBRUARY 10

1942: Lieutenant Gordon Houston of the U.S. Army Air Corps becomes the first professional player killed in World War II when his training plane crashes near Tacoma, Washington. Houston, an outfielder, had played for the league's Oklahoma City Indians in 1938.

FEBRUARY 11

1888: The Dallas club in the newly formed Texas League announces it will have new grandstands—"in the style of the Philadelphia Baseball Park"—built and ready to go by March 17, when the famed Cincinnati club from the American Association would be in town for a pair of exhibition games.

March

MARCH 15

1993: Paul Easterling, the Texas League career leader in games played, runs, hits, extra-base hits, total bases, doubles, home runs and RBIs, dies in Reidsville, Georgia, at the age of eighty-seven. Easterling, who appeared in the Major Leagues briefly in 1928, '30 and '38, played in the Texas League for thirteen seasons with five different teams.

MARCH 18

1888: Teams scheduled to begin the Texas League's first season announce their rosters, as well as the color schemes for their uniforms. Austin was old gold and maroon, Dallas was maroon and white, Fort Worth was blue and white, Galveston was blue and maroon and Houston was bottle green and maroon. San Antonio did not provide a roster or a color scheme.

MARCH 19

1952: The Dallas Eagles release thirty-one-year-old second baseman Ray Neil, the first African American player signed by a Texas League organization. Neil, who played in the Negro Leagues in the 1940s, never appeared in a Texas League game.

MARCH 25

1958: Clarence "Big Boy" Kraft, one of the league's greatest sluggers, dies in Fort Worth at the age of seventy. Kraft drove in 196 runs and hit fifty-five home runs in 1924 and then retired to go into the automobile business in Fort Worth. His single-season RBI record has never been matched, and the home run mark stood for thirty years.

Clarence "Big Boy" Kraft was the league's elite power hitter during the early twentieth century. *Photo Courtesy Bain News Service Archives, Library of Congress.*

April

April 1

1888: In front of a crowd estimated at two thousand, the Houston Babies top the Galveston Giants 4–1 in the first game in league history. The first hit was a single by Galveston second baseman Joe Dowie in the second inning. Dowie went on to play pro baseball for sixteen more seasons, most of them in his hometown of New Orleans.

April 2

1949: Fort Worth becomes the first league team to appear on television as WBAP broadcasts the Cats' exhibition game against their parent club, the Brooklyn Dodgers. The Dodgers, who went on to claim the National League pennant, won 9–3.

2009: San Antonio's Seth Johnston hits a grand slam in the first inning as the Missions beat the San Diego Padres 7–3 at Wolff Stadium. On the same night, Corpus Christi topped the Houston Astros 6–5 at Whataburger Field in front of a record crowd of 9,118.

APRIL 3

1977: Portions of Tulsa's forty-three-year-old ballpark, built entirely from wood by the Works Progress Administration in 1934, succumb to the elements during an exhibition game between the Houston Astros and Texas Rangers. Still, the Drillers found a way to stay at the old stadium through the 1980 season.

2003: Midland's Rich Harden throws six perfect innings in the RockHounds' 5–0 victory over Round Rock. In his next start, Harden threw seven perfect innings, and he was then promoted to Triple-A. He was pitching for the Oakland Athletics before the end of July.

APRIL 4

1998: San Antonio's Angel Pena drives in six runs with a single, a triple and a home run in a victory over Midland. Two days later, Pena

Top: Rich Harden started the 2003 season in Midland but was in the Major Leagues by July. *Courtesy Midland RockHounds.*

Right: San Antonio's Angel Pena had the best year of his career in 1998. *Photo by Jim Vasaldua.*

went five for five, hitting for the cycle in a game at El Paso. The catcher had the best season of his career in 1998, hitting .335 with thirty-two doubles, twenty-two homers and 105 RBIs.

APRIL 6

Troy Glaus started the 1998 season in the Texas League and finished it in the Majors. *Texas League collection.*

1888: Galveston pitcher W.F. Wehrle throws the first shutout in league history, blanking Dallas 3–0 on just one hit. Wehrle's catcher that day was twenty-year-old "Gentleman" George Stallings, who twenty-six years later would become famous as the manager of the 1914 "Miracle" Boston Braves.

1998: Midland third baseman Troy Glaus hits two homers as the Angels pound Wichita 14–9. The shots gave Glaus five in his first five games as a pro, along with thirteen RBIs. Glaus was in the Anaheim Angels' lineup by the end of the 1998 season, on his way to a thirteen-year career in the Majors.

2001: Four Round Rock pitchers combine to strike out 19 Midland hitters, led by 11 from Brad Lidge. Six days later, the Express did it again. Starter Carlos Hernandez struck out 13 El Paso batters in the first six innings, and Jeriome Robertson added 6 more in the last three. Not surprisingly, Round Rock led the league in strikeouts (1,138) and also had a league-high seventeen shutouts and a league-low 3.62 ERA in 2001.

APRIL 7

1899: John Douglas becomes the first Texas college player to appear in a professional game. The University of Texas student, pitching for Austin, shut out San Antonio 4–0. It was Douglas's only appearance as a pro.

APRIL 8

1997: Homer Peel, who played parts of fourteen seasons in the Texas League and has the top career batting average in league history at .325, dies at the age of ninety-four in Shreveport, Louisiana. Peel was known as the "Ty Cobb of the Texas League," as he topped .300 in eight seasons.

Homer Peel owns the top career batting average in league history, .325. *Texas League collection.*

1999: In their first game under their new nickname and as an affiliate of the Oakland A's, the Midland RockHounds get consecutive home runs in the sixth inning by Mario Encarnacion, Justin Bowles and Adam Piatt and roll to a 7–2 decision over San Antonio.

APRIL 9

1889: The second Texas League season gets off to a controversial start as the San Antonio Bronchos are awarded a 9–0 forfeit over the Austin Terrors. The trouble began when Austin's Fred Valdois was ejected for arguing with umpire Ed Clark and continued when Terrors manager/first baseman Mike O'Connor was tossed from the game moments later. With the two ejections, Austin—leading 5–2 at the time—did not have enough players to continue.

1953: Chuck Harmon, the first African American player for Tulsa, drives in both runs as Tulsa blanks Oklahoma City 2–0. Harmon went on to hit .311 in 1953.

1982: Jackson outfielder Darryl Strawberry hits for the cycle in his Double-A debut as the Mets beat Tulsa 14–4. Strawberry doubled in the second, tripled in the fourth, walked in the fifth, homered in the seventh and singled in the eighth.

Darryl Strawberry hit for the cycle in his Texas League debut for Jackson. *Texas League collection.*

APRIL 10

1889: Austin second baseman Harry Truby and first baseman Mike O'Connor combine for the first triple play in league history, turning it against Galveston.

1935: Beaumont beats Houston 2–1 in seventy-five minutes. It was the fastest game ever played at Beaumont's Stuart Stadium and one of the shortest in league history.

1948: Flamboyant East Texas oilman R.W. "Dick" Burnett buys the Dallas Eagles for $500,000 just days before the season opener. Burnett began a noteworthy term as an owner by announcing he had been in contact with the owners of several teams in the Pacific Coast League about forming a third major league.

1994: For just the second time in league history, two no-hitters are recorded on the same night—both by visiting pitchers. In Shreveport, Arkansas left-hander Rigo Beltran beat the Captains 2–0, striking out six and walking two. In Tulsa, Jackson's Kevin Gallaher and Jimmy Daspit combined to pitch a seven-inning no-hitter, winning 3–0. The only other time there were two no-hitters on the same day was June 26, 1906.

2008: An overflow crowd of 7,820 sees the first Texas League game at Arvest Ballpark as San Antonio tops Northwest Arkansas 7–1. It took community leaders in Springdale, Arkansas, more than six and a half years to bring a team to the region.

APRIL 11

1920: Deciding the nickname Aces was bad luck, the San Antonio team changes its name to the Bears, a play on words since San Antonio is in Bexar (which is pronounced like "bear") County.

1936: Japan's top baseball team, the Tokyo Giants, edges the Tulsa Oilers 9–8. The Giants had seven hits and worked the Drillers for six walks. Tulsa won 3–1 the next day.

1950: Dallas sets the league single-game attendance record—which still stands—by putting 53,578 fans into the Cotton Bowl for a game against Tulsa. The main attraction was the starting lineup for the Eagles, a collection of retired big-league stars, including Ty Cobb, Tris Speaker, Duffy Lewis, Dizzy Dean, Mickey Cochrane, Charlie Gehringer, Travis Jackson and Frank "Home Run" Baker.

APRIL 12

1898: Thanks to a soggy field, Austin and Galveston commit six errors each. Not surprisingly, considering all the free base runners, the final score was 21–13 in favor of Austin.

1930: On a wild night in Waco, the Cubs' Gene Rye hits three home runs and goes five for six in a 15–5 victory over San Antonio. Waco's Charles Stuvengen walked five times, a league record.

APRIL 13

1932: San Antonio achieves a league record for frustration, leaving fifteen runners on base in a 12–1 loss to Beaumont.

1949: Dallas collects twenty-six hits in a 23–2 romp over Oklahoma City. The team was led by third baseman Bill Serena, who had seven RBIs. Serena, a .278 lifetime hitter, had a single, a double and two home runs. He was one of five Dallas hitters to have at least four hits in the game.

1953: Harry Wilson, the first African American pitcher in San Antonio, wins his debut with a 2–1, ten-inning victory. Wilson walked five batters and gave up ten hits, but he also went two for four at the plate and had a single in the tenth inning to start the game-winning rally.

1956: Shreveport cleanup hitter Dale Coogan knocks in seven runs with a two-run homer in the first, a two-run triple in the third and a three-run homer in the fourth as the Sports win 14–12.

1981: Brothers Steve Sax and Dave Sax each hit three-run homers during a ten-run seventh inning, leading San Antonio's 34–8 romp over Midland. Steve finished the season in the big leagues and stayed for thirteen more years; Dave appeared in thirty-seven games in the Majors from 1982 to 1987.

1998: El Paso leadoff hitter Anthony Iapoce homers to start the game, and it would be the only run the Diablos would need in a 1–0 victory over San Antonio.

Left-hander Andy Pratt tossed a no-hitter for Tulsa in 2001. *Photo by Tom Kayser.*

2001: Tulsa left-hander Andy Pratt throws the first no-hitter of his life as the Drillers top Arkansas 1–0 in the first game of a double-header. Pratt finished the seven-inning game with two walks and eleven strikeouts, but he was just 8-10 with a 4.61 ERA for the 2001 season.

APRIL 14

1911: Oklahoma City scores thirteen runs in the seventh inning, rallying to beat Dallas 16–11.

1952: Pitcher Dave Hoskins, the first African American player in league history, gives up two runs and eight hits in Dallas's 4–2 victory over Tulsa. Hoskins finished the season with a league-best twenty-two victories and a 2.12 ERA.

1956: Shreveport's Ken Guettler begins one of the more improbable slugging explosions in league history by hitting three home runs in an 11–9 loss to Houston. Guettler would finish the season with sixty-two homers, a mark that still stands.

Dallas's Dave
Hoskins,
the league's
first African
American player.
*Courtesy Dallas
Public Library.*

1960: A much-hyped bid for back-to-back no-hitters in Austin ends on the game's second pitch. The Senators' Charlie Gorin had finished the 1959 season with a no-hitter, and preseason advertising promoted his bid to duplicate the feat. But San Antonio leadoff man J.C. Hartman fouled off the first pitch and doubled to left field on the second. Gorin went on to win anyway.

1967: Austin pitcher Jim Britton comes within a first-inning walk of a perfect game and strikes out fifteen in a 3–0 victory over Arkansas to start the season. Britton was just 1-3 in six starts for Austin, but he wound up the season in Triple-A.

FAST START

El Paso's John Jaha had a hit in nineteen of his first twenty-six at-bats in the league in 1991, posting a .537 batting average with twenty RBIs. He posted at least one hit in each of his first eleven games, including a four-for-four night on April 12 and a five-for-five night on April 14.

John Jaha hit .537 in his first twenty-six at-bats for El Paso in 1991. *Texas League collection.*

APRIL 15

1941: Dallas, which lost its ballpark to a fire at the end of the 1940 season, opens 1941 with a 13–5 loss to Fort Worth in a game played in Waco. It was the first Texas League game in Waco in almost eleven years.

1956: San Antonio scores seven runs in the first and fourth innings but needs two more in the eighth to hold off Austin 20–18. The teams combine for thirty-eight hits, including a record seventeen doubles.

1972: As players in the Major Leagues return from a short strike, the four-man grounds crew at Memphis starts their own. Demanding a pay raise, they staged a sit-down strike before the game.

Luis Raven blasted eighteen homers and fifty-seven RBIs in just forty-seven Texas League games in 1994. *Texas League collection.*

1972: Midland makes its debut in the Texas League with a 5–2 victory at San Antonio. The Cubs broke up a no-hitter in the fifth inning and then scored all their runs in a five-run outburst in the eighth.

1977: Jackson's John Pacella walks six and hits two batters but doesn't give up a hit in a 3–0 victory over Tulsa. It was the highlight of a season that saw him go 10-9 in Class A and Double-A.

1990: Scoring in every inning but the seventh, the San Antonio Missions pound out 21 hits to beat El Paso 19–9. Eric Karros led the Missions with 4 hits, launching a season that would see him lead the league in batting average (.352), hits (179), doubles (45), extra-base hits (65) and total bases (282).

1994: Midland's Luis Raven strokes two homers and drives in five runs in the Angels' 13–7 victory over El Paso. The twenty-six-year-old native of Venezuela would go on to hit eighteen homers with fifty-seven RBIs in forty-seven Texas League games before being promoted to Triple-A.

APRIL 16

1917: Shreveport's Dixie Carroll singles in the winning run in the bottom of the seventeenth inning, making a loser of Fort Worth's Fritz Redford. Both Redford and Shreveport's Ollie Jost pitched all seventeen innings.

1920: Wichita Falls makes its Texas League debut by scoring a run in the bottom of the ninth to edge Dallas 2–1. Clubs from the north Texas city went on to go 1,061-833, the best winning percentage (.560) for a team with at least 1,000 Texas League victories.

1932: Five pitchers walk five men each in Wichita Falls' 9–6 victory over Shreveport. The league record for walks is twenty-six, set on August 21, 1923.

1953: Oklahoma City scores twelve runs in the first inning of a game with Fort Worth but is shut out the rest of the way. The Indians hung on for a 12–9 victory.

1968: The Texas League returns to San Antonio after a four-year absence as the Missions beat Amarillo 3–2 in ten innings. A crowd of 3,037 filled V.J. Keefe Field at the beginning of a unique partnership between the minor-league team and St. Mary's University, where the field was located.

1968: Pro baseball comes back to Memphis as 5,447 show up to see the first contest in the city since 1961.

1989: Arkansas center fielder Ray Lankford hits for the cycle in the Travelers' 21–7 romp over Tulsa. Lankford would make his Major League debut in 1990 and wound up playing fourteen seasons in the big leagues.

2000: The league returns to the Austin area for the first time since the 1960s with the opening of Round Rock's Dell Diamond. An overflow crowd of

The Texas League returned to San Antonio in 1968 at V.J. Keefe Field. *Texas League collection.*

Keith Ginter hit the first home run in Round Rock history. *Photo by Tom Kayser.*

10,699 also saw the first homer in Round Rock history, a four-hundred-foot shot by second baseman Keith Ginter in the first inning.

2006: Midland scores in every inning of a 20–10 blowout of Corpus Christi. The team was led by Jason Perry, who hit for the cycle, and Kevin Melillo, who went six for seven. Every batter in the RockHounds' lineup had at least one hit.

2011: Arkansas steals eight bases, including five in the fourth inning, during a 10–2 victory over Midland.

PACKING THEM IN

Round Rock holds the top four spots in the record book for single-season attendance, including a Double-A record 689,286 in 2004. The Express also had the best single-season marks for 2000–03.

An overflow crowd fills the Dell Diamond in Round Rock in 2000. *Texas League collection.*

APRIL 17

1915: The league's first infield tarp, proudly billed as 2,300 yards of canvas, is unveiled by Dallas owner/president Joseph W. Gardner.

1931: Shreveport and Dallas play to a 9–9 tie in a game marked by a fight involving Sports third baseman Jim Vorhoff and Dallas player/manager Hap Morse, an eight-run Dallas rally in the fourth and a two-run, game-tying homer in the seventh.

1935: Oklahoma City shortstop Louis Brower walks in four consecutive at-bats, singles and steals three bases in a 14–2 thumping of Dallas. Brower's last stolen base was home.

1972: Three Arkansas pitchers strike out thirteen and walk just one, but the Travelers still lose to Memphis, 8–4.

1978: El Paso and Midland combine to leave thirty-two men on base in the Diablos' 9–4 victory. There were twenty-four walks and twenty hits in the game as well.

1985: Center fielder Ruben Sierra has just one hit but drives in five runs in a 12–7 victory over Arkansas. Sierra ripped a three-run homer in the first inning and drove in runs with a sacrifice fly and a groundout. "El Caballo" was a four-time All-Star in the Majors and finished second in MVP voting in 1989, when he led the American League with 119 RBI, fourteen triples and a .543 slugging percentage for the Texas Rangers.

APRIL 18

1898: Houston's Bill Kemmer sets a hitting record that still stands, driving in twelve runs in his team's 16–10 victory over Fort Worth. Kemmer had two singles and three three-run home runs. The first baseman played seventeen seasons in the minor leagues and appeared in eleven games for Louisville in the National League in 1895.

1898: After three shutout innings by San Antonio pitcher Jake Volz, Galveston explodes for sixteen runs in its final six innings, cruising to a 16–3 victory. Volz walked ten, hit two batters and delivered three wild pitches in taking the loss.

1915: Dode Criss, the Houston Buffs' regular first baseman, throws the second no-hitter of his career, beating San Antonio 3–0. Criss was one of the league's greatest all-around players, with a career batting average of .308 in the minors and ninety-three victories as a pitcher.

1947: More than four thousand fans, equipped with cushions and folding chairs, crowd the foul lines of unfinished Mission Stadium to see Beaumont top San Antonio 8–7 in the Missions' home opener. The ballpark, designed to seat fourteen thousand, was completed five weeks later.

1948: Tulsa collects twenty-seven hits in a 31–1 thrashing of Dallas. Russ Burns connected for three home runs and a triple, scoring six runs and driving in seven. Third baseman Tommy Tatum also drove in seven runs.

Tulsa's Russ Burns hit three homers and drove in seven runs for the Oilers on April 18, 1948. *Texas League collection.*

1959: Austin's Gerald Mason drives in six runs with just two hits in a 14–2 blowout of Tulsa. Mason had a bases-loaded triple in the fourth and a three-run homer in the seventh. Oddly, Mason had just eight other hits in eighteen games for the Senators in 1959; he spent most of the season at Class-B Wenatchee, where he hit .356 and drove in seventy runs.

1965: League president Hugh Finnerty is pressed into duty when Albuquerque broadcaster Ed Mueller loses his voice from laryngitis. Finnerty had been a radio broadcaster before his career in baseball.

1969: Dallas–Fort Worth catcher Johnny Oates hits the first inside-the-park homer in Turnpike Stadium history, driving in Larry Johnson with what proves to be the winning runs in a 2–1 decision over Albuquerque. Twenty-six years later, Oates returned to Arlington as the manager of the Texas Rangers.

1991: Tulsa pitchers Cedric Shaw, Everett Cunningham and Barry Manuel combine for a 2–0, no-hit win over Arkansas. Shaw pitched the first seven innings, walking six.

1994: In what would become a pattern of low-scoring games at the ballpark, El Paso tops San Antonio 1–0 in the first game at the Missions' new Wolff Stadium.

2002: The Arkansas Travelers bat around in two different innings in a 13–4 pounding of Tulsa. The Travs put up a five-run first inning and a seven-run eighth.

APRIL 19

1909: Ten minutes after a fire destroys half his ballpark, Galveston owner Joseph Gardner is on the phone ordering lumber and arranging for a work crew. The team played a home game the next day, and the burned-out section of grandstands, nearly 1,800 seats, was completely replaced in two days.

1917: Waco pitcher Jimmy Zinn, who had been left home to work himself into shape, rushes to Fort Worth when scheduled starter Clarence Simms gets sick. Zinn wound up throwing a no-hitter in a 4–0 victory over the Cats and wound up winning fourteen games in 1917.

1917: Opposing pitchers Snipe Conley of Dallas and Joe Gleason of Shreveport both throw two-hitters. Gleason did not give up a hit until two outs in the seventh, when Peaches Crouch doubled. Eddie Palmer followed with a single, driving in the only run of the game.

1920: San Antonio's Pete Knisely becomes the first player to homer over the deep center-field wall at his club's League Park. The ball hit the ground twenty feet in front of the wall and bounced over, which under the rules of the day made it a home run.

1961: Tulsa second baseman Jack Damaska leads off the game against Amarillo with a home run and then singles in the winning run ten innings later as the Oilers triumph 7–6.

1964: Fort Worth left-hander Loyd Wallis pays the price for breaking a cardinal rule of baseball. With two men on base, Tulsa pitcher Otto Meischner bunted. Wallis threw his glove at the ball, and under the rules, the umpires awarded Meischner three bases. (Wallis should have known better—he had been playing pro ball since 1950.)

1968: Arkansas pitcher Felix Roque wins the first game of a double-header with Memphis and then loses the second game. He was called into the nightcap when the Travelers ran out of pitchers in the sixteenth inning and gave up three runs. Roque finished the season 1–1 in thirteen appearances for the Travelers.

1972: The Midland Cubs miss batting practice in their home debut in the Texas League when club employees cannot find the key to the shed where the batting practice balls are stored. The Cubs also suffered through a windstorm and a rain delay in the first professional baseball game in the city since 1959.

1999: Adam Piatt goes five for five with three doubles, one home run and 5 RBIs as Midland opens its first season as an affiliate of the Oakland A's with a 10–2 victory over El Paso. Piatt would go on to win the Texas League Triple Crown, hitting .345 with thirty-nine homers and 135 RBIs.

2011: Frisco's Martin Perez does not allow a base runner through five innings, and when the RoughRiders' game at Arkansas ends because of rain in the sixth inning, he gets credit for a perfect game. The left-hander struck out three in the 1–0 victory.

TRIPLE THREAT

Adam Piatt recorded the first Triple Crown in the league in seventy-two seasons in 1999, hitting .345 with 39 homers and 135 RBIs. Piatt, in just his third year of professional baseball, also led the league in runs scored (128, 28 more than the second-place finisher), total bases (335, the highest total in forty-five years), walks (tied at 93), on-base percentage (.451), extra-base hits (90) and slugging percentage (.704, just the fourth player to lead the Texas League with a mark above .700). The other Triple Crowns were won by Waco's Del Pratt in 1927 (.386/32/140) and Northwest Arkansas' Clint Robinson in 2010 (.335/29/98).

Three pitchers have won the equivalent Triple Crown, leading the league in victories, ERA and strikeouts. The first was San Antonio's Sid Fernandez in 1983. Fernandez won a league-high thirteen games with 209

Adam Piatt won the Texas League Triple Crown in 1999. *Photo by Tom Kayser.*

Shreveport's George Ferran led the league in victories, ERA and strikeouts in 1986. *Texas League collection.*

33

strikeouts and an ERA of 2.28. Shreveport's George Ferran did it in 1986, and Tulsa's Samuel Deduno accomplished the feat in 2009.

APRIL 20

1898: Just three days after being pounded for fifteen hits by Galveston, San Antonio pitcher Jake Volz beats Austin 1–0, allowing just one hit. "Silent Jake," a native of San Antonio, went on to play until 1909 and was the first San Antonian to reach the Majors when he debuted with the Boston Americans in 1901.

1947: Oklahoma City pulls off one of the rarest feats in baseball history, a triple steal, in an exhibition game against the Cleveland Indians. OKC's Al Rosen slid home with the run on the play, to the delight of a crowd of 7,696. Rosen went on to hit .349 and was named the Texas League MVP in 1947.

1950: Emil Tellinger of Beaumont ties a league record, hitting into three double plays against Shreveport.

1959: The only thing that stops Austin in a 17–4 victory in Amarillo is the weather. The game was called because of rain and snow just as the Senators scored nine runs in the seventh inning.

1960: Tulsa rookie pitcher Fred Walker walks the first four hitters of his team's game against Austin but doesn't give up a run. Leadoff man Pepper Thomas was thrown out trying to steal, and after three straight walks, Walker struck out the next two batters.

1969: In the first game of a double-header, Memphis left-hander Les Rohr throws a no-hitter, beating San Antonio 8–0. Rohr, the second player taken overall in the 1965 draft, had earned a spot in baseball history the previous year as the losing pitcher in the twenty-four-inning game between the Mets and the Houston Astros.

1989: Tulsa leadoff hitter Sammy Sosa hits a three-run homer in the twelfth inning, giving the Drillers an 11–8 decision over Jackson. Sosa would finish the season in the Majors and go on to play in the big leagues until 2007.

APRIL 21

1947: Shreveport's Bob Prichard drives in seven runs in a 14–8 victory over San Antonio—after entering the game in the fifth inning. Prichard started a four-for-four day with a pinch-hit single, and he also had two triples.

1949: Harry Donabedian of Tulsa ties a league record by walking five times—against five different pitchers—in the Oilers' 10–7 victory at Oklahoma City. The Tulsa shortstop had no official at-bats, as he was credited with a sacrifice in his only other plate appearance.

1955: An opponent finally keeps San Antonio's Carl Powis off base after he had reached thirteen times in a row. Powis singled in his only plate appearance on April 19. He had a walk, a single, a double and a home run in the first game of a double-header on the twentieth, and he walked four times and singled twice in the second game. On the twenty-first, he was hit by a pitch and walked before Shreveport finally sent him back to the dugout.

Tulsa's Harry Donabedian walked five times against five different Oklahoma City pitchers on April 21, 1949. *Texas League collection.*

1966: Amarillo's Don Wilson pitches his second shutout in as many starts, beating El Paso 9–0 while allowing six hits and striking out twelve. He had given up four hits in shutting out Dallas–Fort Worth in his Texas League debut four days earlier. Wilson went on to throw two no-hitters for the Houston Astros and won 104 games in nine seasons.

1977: Tulsa's Billy Sample hits for the cycle in the Drillers' 13–3 romp over Arkansas. Sample tripled in the first, hit a two-run homer in the fifth, doubled in the eighth and singled in the ninth.

1996: Wichita catcher Andy Stewart steals home in a 4–1 victory over San Antonio. The not-too-fleet Stewart had two other stolen bases in 1996 and twenty-four total in eleven minor-league seasons.

APRIL 22

1921: Fort Worth first baseman Clarence "Big Boy" Kraft goes five for five with a double and three homers as the Cats hold off Wichita Falls 14–11.

1975: Midland records one off the oddest triple plays in league history. With runners at first and second, Shreveport's Ken Melvin grounded into what seemed like a routine double play. Apparently thinking the inning was over, Midland shortstop Mike Sembler and catcher Ed Putnam headed for the dugout. So Shreveport's Mitchell Page, who was standing on third base, broke for the plate. Putnam recovered just in time to take a throw from first baseman Aaron Randall and tag out Page.

2011: San Antonio's Jaff Decker joins a select group of players, striking out 5 times in a nine-inning game. Only eight others have whiffed 5 times in a single contest in league history. Decker wound up with 145 strikeouts for the season, but he also walked 103 times.

APRIL 23

1925: The San Antonio Bears get amazing production from their right fielders in a 21–1 romp over Beaumont. Sy Rosenthal, who started the game, had two home runs and a triple in three trips to the plate. His replacement, Lymon Nason, had two singles and two triples in four times at the plate.

1930: Oscar "Ox" Eckhardt, a year and a half removed from a season of pro football with the New York Giants, goes six for six to lead Beaumont's 17–4 rout of Waco. Eckhardt, a multi-sport standout at the University of Texas, played professional baseball on and off from 1925 to 1940.

1965: The Dallas–Fort Worth area returns to the Texas League as the Spurs shut out Amarillo 4–0. The opening of the new Turnpike Stadium in Arlington attracted a crowd of 7,231.

1969: Dusty Baker's grand slam in the bottom of the eighth inning accounts for all the scoring in Shreveport's 4–0 victory over El Paso. Baker wound up playing parts of nineteen seasons in the Major Leagues, hitting 242 homers, and has been a big-league manager on and off from 1993 through 2013.

2011: San Antonio scores twenty runs for the third time in twelve days, rolling over Midland 21–8. Jaff Decker drove in seven for the Missions after having struck out five times the previous night.

Future big-league player and manager Dusty Baker, who played for the Shreveport Braves in 1969. *Texas League collection.*

APRIL 24

1951: Dallas pitcher Ray Narleski flirts with disaster all night against Tulsa, walking nine and hitting a batter in his Texas League debut. He still won, 2–0, thanks to the fact that he allowed just one hit, to the second batter of the game.

1954: Fort Worth first baseman Gabe Gabler drives in ten runs in three successive innings, leading the Cats to a 20–4 romp over Beaumont. After singling in the fifth, Gabler cleaned the bases with a three-run double in the sixth, hit a three-run homer in the seventh and then launched a grand slam in the eighth.

1968: San Antonio pounds El Paso 10–0 using just three swings of the bat to score all ten runs. Outfielder George Pena hit a first-inning grand slam, and Garry Jestadt and Ken Rudolph each ripped three-run home runs later in the game. Jestadt went on to be part of a footnote in baseball history, playing in six games for the Montreal Expos in 1969, the club's National League debut season. Rudolph appeared in twenty-seven games for the star-crossed Chicago Cubs that year and wound up playing parts of nine seasons in the Majors.

1998: Midland rallies from a 16–4 deficit with a thirteen-run seventh inning but falls 19–17 when El Paso scores two more in the bottom half of the inning. The teams combined for forty hits.

APRIL 25

1898: San Antonio and Austin pair up for one of the sloppiest games in league history as they record nineteen errors by thirteen different players. San Antonio, which had nine of the miscues, won 24–12.

1928: Les Cox pitches all twelve innings of San Antonio's 1–0 victory over Houston but does not get credit for a complete game. Cox entered the game in the first inning with the bases loaded and nobody out, and his first pitch resulted in a triple play. He allowed five hits the rest of the game, which San Antonio took on Dusty Boggess's run-scoring double.

1941: Houston's nineteen-year-old left-hander Howie Pollet runs his scoreless innings streak to eighteen in a 7–0 no-hitter against Shreveport. Pollet would finish the season 20-3 with a 1.16 ERA and was sent up to the St. Louis Cardinals—the first of his nineteen seasons in the Majors, where he won 131 games.

1949: Dallas loses for the first time in 1949, falling to Tulsa 12–3 after starting the season 11-0.

1953: Fort Worth's Leonard Lamont comes to the plate three times with the bases loaded in a 15–4 victory at Houston. He hit a grand slam in the first inning and a two-run double in the second, with the ball hitting high off the left-field wall. The third time? Lamont struck out. The six RBIs were 60 percent of his total for his sixteen games in 1953, his last season in baseball.

1970: El Paso puts up single runs in each inning and winds up with a 10–9 victory over Shreveport in ten innings.

2001: Round Rock pitchers piece together their second one-hitter in a row, beating Tulsa 1–0. Tim Redding and Brandon Puffer combined for a 6–1 victory the day before, and Doug Sessions, Jeriome Robertson and Travis Wade teamed up on April 25. Tulsa's only hit in the second game was by the first batter of the game.

APRIL 26

1914: Waco's Hatton "The Professor" Ogle pitches a 6–0 no-hitter over the hapless Austin Senators. The game's lone umpire, F.E. Muir, was knocked off his feet by a pickoff by Austin pitcher Jake Smith. (Muir was at his customary spot, no more than six feet behind the mound.)

1967: Albuquerque scores nine runs on just two hits in the first four innings of an 18–3 romp over Arkansas. Travelers pitchers walked eleven, recorded three wild pitches and were also charged with a balk. Not being much help, Arkansas' defense committed three errors.

APRIL 27

1950: Four Fort Worth batters reach base safely in the seventh inning of a 5–1 victory over San Antonio—and none of them gets past second base. After a single and a walk to start the inning, Missions pitcher Hal Hudson picked Frank Brown off second base for the first out. Following an error, Hudson picked Dick Williams off second. And following another hit, Hudson trapped Joe Torpey off second to end the inning. Williams went on to play thirteen seasons in the big leagues and manage for twenty-one years, earning election to the National Baseball Hall of Fame in 2008.

1966: Austin pitcher Pat House drives in eight runs in a 19–4 romp over El Paso. House had two two-run doubles, an RBI single and three run-scoring groundouts. He finished the season with a career-best .218 batting average.

1992: El Paso pitchers David Martinez, Jeff Tabaka and Rob Wishnevski combine to strike out seventeen San Antonio hitters in a 7–2 victory. Martinez had eight in five innings, and Tabaka struck out eight in three innings.

APRIL 28

1906: Carl Hiatt opens Waco's season with a 2–0 no-hitter against Temple. It was the first no-hitter at Waco's Katy Park and the highlight of Hiatt's season. He went 8-17 in twenty-seven games.

1914: Dallas releases eighteen-year-old rookie Rogers Hornsby following a tryout. Hornsby caught on with Hugo in the Texas-Oklahoma League but was released to Denison of the same league on July 2. Hornsby started the 1915 season with Denison but finished it with the St. Louis Cardinals—the first of his twenty-three seasons in the big leagues, on the way to the National Baseball Hall of Fame.

1925: Joe Pate of Fort Worth and Bob Osborn of Wichita Falls pitch every inning of a scoreless fourteen-inning tie in Wichita Falls. Pate held the Spudders to six hits, with three walks and six strikeouts. Osborn allowed the Cats five hits while walking four and striking out eight.

1931: Beaumont's Stuart Stadium, one of the few concrete-and-steel ballparks in the state, is formally dedicated—three years after it opened. The occasion was a visit from Commissioner Kenesaw Mountain Landis, who participated in the ceremonies.

1937: Tulsa's game at Galveston is called off for the second night in a row because of heavy fog.

1949: Pete Gray, the one-armed outfielder who had played in the Major Leagues during World War II, has four hits, scores two runs, steals a base and drives in a run for Dallas. The 1949 season turned out to be Gray's last in baseball; he hit .214 in forty-five games for the Eagles.

1974: Shreveport sends sixteen men to the plate in the third inning, an eleven-run outburst that results in a 14–5 pasting of Alexandria. Tom Stedman, Duane Espy and Gary Martz each recorded two hits and two RBIs in the inning.

1990: Wichita pummels Midland 33–17, with the teams combining for forty-nine hits. Catcher Dan Walters and first baseman Guillermo Velasquez each had five hits, and every Wichita hitter scored at least twice.

APRIL 29

1960: San Antonio and Rio Grande Valley set the record for the longest game in league history, 24 innings. With fog creeping in at Mission Stadium, the Giants scored twice in the top of the 24th for a 4–2 victory. The game took five hours and forty-two minutes to play and ended at 1:27 a.m. Rio Grande Valley pitcher Bob Bolin got the victory with 9.2 innings of relief. Bill Valentine, who would go on to umpire in the American League and later run the Arkansas Travelers for more than thirty years, was the home-plate umpire the entire game.

Mike Lutz had three hits in his final game in pro baseball. *Texas League collection.*

1960: Austin's Mike Lutz goes out with three hits, including a home run, in a double-header against Tulsa. The thirty-two-year-old Lutz had announced he was retiring to become a deputy sheriff in Warren, Ohio.

41

Cotton Nash was an All-American basketball player at Kentucky. *Texas League collection.*

1965: Cotton Nash, a basketball All-American at Kentucky, goes five for seven and drives in the winning run in a twelve-inning, 12–11 victory over Amarillo. Amarillo outfielder Brock Davis hit for the cycle and drove in three runs as well.

1989: Andy Benes pitches his third consecutive shutout, topping Midland 9–0. In twenty-seven innings, Benes allowed just eight hits and five walks, with thirty-nine strikeouts. Benes went 8-4 with a 2.16 ERA for Wichita before earning a promotion to Triple-A.

2010: Arkansas' Ryan Brasier throws the first nine-inning no-hitter in the Texas League since 2002, stifling Tulsa 4–0. The former reliever's gem was the first no-hitter at Dickey-Stephens Park.

Wichita pitcher Andy Benes went 8-4 with a 2.16 ERA in 1989. *Texas League collection.*

April 30

1924: Fort Worth Cats first baseman Clarence "Big Boy" Kraft starts a ten-game streak during which he has nineteen hits in thirty-two at-bats with eight home runs, fifteen runs and nineteen RBIs. The Cats won nine of the ten games during the streak.

1930: Fort Worth outfielder Eddie Moore's streak of 573 consecutive games played ends when he is called home because of a death in the family. The streak began in 1926.

1966: Pitching in relief, Amarillo right-hander Ron Cayll strikes out 7 consecutive El Paso batters in a 9–4 victory. In eleven seasons in the minors, Cayll struck out 635 batters, including 182 for Oklahoma City and Amarillo in 1965.

1983: El Paso outslugs Beaumont 35–21 in one of the highest-scoring games in minor-league history. The teams record 56 hits, including 38 singles. El Paso's Mike Felder drove in nine runs with a grand slam, a three-run homer, a sacrifice fly and a bunt. It was part of a day on which league teams scored ninety-two runs and collected 123 hits. (Beaumont had its revenge the next night, winning 20–13.)

1994: El Paso left fielder Danny Perez ties a league record with three triples in the Diablos' 9–2 victory over Midland. The three-triple game was the fifteenth in league history but the first since 1947. Perez finished the season with seventeen triples, tops in the league and in his career.

May

MAY 1

1910: Oklahoma City's Henry Chelette pitches a no-hitter, stifling Waco 7–0. Chelette went on to win twenty-one games in 1910 and twenty-seven for St. Joseph in the Western League in 1911.

1930: Texas League owners vote unanimously to rescind a league rule barring radio broadcasts of games.

1960: Despite issuing thirteen walks, Victoria pitchers cruise to an 11–5 victory over Austin.

1991: Jackson pitchers walk 14 Shreveport hitters and give up eleven hits in a 17–5 loss. Jackson's Kevin Coffman walked 6 and gave up five runs on just one hit in the sixth inning. Coffman wound up walking 101 in 105.2 innings in 1991, to go with his 105 strikeouts.

1996: Wichita second baseman Jed Hansen goes three for three with three extra-base hits, three runs and three RBIs in a 7–5 decision over El Paso.

2007: Drew Macias and Sean Kazmar both hit grand slams during San Antonio's nine-run sixth inning as the Missions blast Frisco 14–6. The homers were the only extra-base hits among San Antonio's seventeen hits on the day.

MAY 2

1953: Dan Stupur and Jim Melton combine to pitch Fort Worth to a 7–2 no-hit victory over Beaumont in the 7-inning nightcap of a double-header. Stupur worked the first 6.1 innings but was pulled after giving up his seventh walk.

1954: San Antonio's Jim Pisoni hits three home runs and drives in eight runs as the Missions blast Fort Worth 20–5. His night included a grand slam in San Antonio's ten-run eighth inning.

1968: Albuquerque's Richard Armstrong fires a no-hitter against Dallas–Fort Worth, walking four and striking out seven in the 10–0 victory. He got hitting support from third baseman Bill Sudakis, who was four for four.

1978: Arkansas pitcher R.J. Harrison gets credit for a no-hitter without getting a decision. After six scoreless innings, the Travelers' game with Jackson was called because of rain. It was the second-longest scoreless no-hitter recorded in league history, as Fort Worth's Harold Christman threw a nine-inning, 0–0 no-hitter against Temple on July 5, 1905.

2000: Big-leaguer Randy Velarde, playing as a pro in his hometown of Midland for the first time, hits a home run in the bottom of the ninth to tie the RockHounds' game with Shreveport at 6. Two innings later, Velarde drew a walk, went to third on a double by Eric Byrnes and scored on a sacrifice fly by Cody McKay as Midland won 7–6.

2006: The first three Tulsa batters hit home runs to left field in a 10–8 victory over Midland. Troy Tulowitzki, Seth Smith and Chris Iannetta started the contest with long balls, and Smith and Iannetta homered again in the second.

2008: Midland's Jon Zeringue raises his batting average twenty-six points in one night, hitting for the cycle in a 9–7 loss to Corpus Christi. Zeringue's final hit, in the bottom of the ninth, was a single.

MAY 3

1899: Three league teams play games in Houston on the same day. Houston's management stops the home club's contest against Austin, charging the players with "indifferent play," and gives refunds to fans. The game was going to be rescheduled for the next day until it was discovered that Austin had to be in San Antonio for a game on May 4. San Antonio happened to be passing through on its way home from Galveston, so the team stopped and played Austin, losing 6–1. Houston and Austin then played the rescheduled contest, with Houston winning 14–10.

1905: Dallas's Charles Porter walks five and has four errors behind him, but he wins by not allowing a hit in a 5–2 decision over Fort Worth. Porter went 10-15 for Dallas in 1905.

1932: Following a loss to the Galveston Buccaneers, Shreveport's Biedenharn Park burns to the ground, taking all the team's equipment. The only casualty was a bird dog owned by Shreveport outfielder George Harper; the dog was housed near the home clubhouse. The franchise played one game in Longview and then moved to Tyler, Texas, on May 6, marking the first time since 1914 that all the league's teams were based in the Lone Star State.

1971: San Antonio's Pat Bourque drives in 8 runs during his team's 14–2 romp past Albuquerque. The season turned out to be the biggest of Bourque's career, as he drove in 128 runs in 129 games in Double-A and Triple-A.

2008: Frisco's Steve Murphy hits two homers and drives in seven runs as the RoughRiders outslug San Antonio 14–10.

MAY 4

1982: El Paso hitters face two Amarillo relief pitchers in the bottom of the tenth but don't see a pitch from either, and the club still winds up with a 16–15 victory. Amarillo reliever Jim Coffman came into the game and sliced his finger trying to clean mud from his spikes before delivering a pitch. Mike Couchee was then brought in and before throwing a pitch made a wild pickoff try at first base. Eric Payton came all the way around to score the winning run.

MAY 5

1913: Waco's Ross Helm, a nineteen-game loser in 1912, stifles Houston with a six-inning no-hitter. His 3–1 victory was shortened by a downpour in the top of the seventh inning. Helm went 14-15 for the Navigators in 1913 and then lost nineteen more for Galveston and Austin in 1914 and promptly retired.

1927: Houston shortstop Eddie Hock pulls off an unassisted triple play, just the second in league history, in a 9–8 loss to Dallas. With runners at first and second in the bottom of the third inning, Hock caught a line drive, stepped on second and then tagged the runner coming from first. It was one of a league-record six triple plays in 1927. (Hock, who was twenty-eight at the time, played pro ball until he was forty-three.)

1933: In the first night games in Dallas history, the Steers sweep a double-header from Oklahoma City, 8–4 and 1–0. Dallas outfielder Tom "Tut" Jenkins collected six consecutive hits, five in the first game.

1948: Shreveport pitcher Red Mann, making his first start of the season, tosses a six-inning no-hitter, blanking Dallas 4–0. The game was stopped in the sixth when high winds and rain swept across the field in Shreveport.

1953: In the first meeting in league history between two African American pitchers, San Antonio's Harry Wilson tops Oklahoma City's Bill Greason 6–1. The game included the first all–African American battery, as Wilson threw to Charley White.

1983: Shreveport's David Wilhelmi pitches the first perfect game in the league since 1935, beating Arkansas

Shreveport's Dave Wilhelmi threw a perfect game against Arkansas in 1983. *Texas League collection.*

7–0. The game was the highlight of a short pro career for the right-hander, who appeared in just 135 games in parts of six seasons, going 38-60 and never advancing beyond Double-A.

1983: El Paso scores thirteen runs in the second inning of a 20–19 slugfest with Midland. Diablos hitters connected on ten consecutive hits and thirteen overall in the inning, with four players each collecting two hits.

MAY 6

Corpus Christi manager Ray Murray used himself as a pinch hitter and started a ten-run inning. *Texas League collection.*

1924: Fort Worth's Clarence "Big Boy" Kraft starts a record run with a homer. He had shots in single games on May 6 and 9 and in both ends of double-headers on May 7–8.

1959: Corpus Christi manager Ray Murray puts himself into the game as a pinch hitter in the seventh inning and launches a ten-run rally. Murray, forty-one, actually batted twice in the big inning, walking his second time up in the 12–8 victory over Austin.

1962: Three consecutive pinch hitters deliver with hits as El Paso rallies past Austin 7–5. Tim Talton, Joe Sparks and Chuck Teuscher delivered successive pinch hits in the eighth.

1965: Amarillo right fielder Charlie Murray hits a three-run homer in the third inning and an inside-the-park grand slam in the fourth in an 11–6 victory at Dallas–Fort Worth.

Arkansas' Bud Smith tossed two no-hitters in 2000. *Photo by Tom Kayser.*

1991: Despite collecting just two hits, Jackson nips Arkansas 1–0 in the second game of a double-header. Generals center fielder Joe Mikulik scored on a bases-loaded walk from Dale Kisten.

1997: Wichita pounds out seventeen hits in a 9–4 victory over Shreveport—fifteen of them by the top four players in the lineup.

2000: Arkansas' Robert "Bud" Smith faces the minimum number of batters in a 5–0 no-hitter against Midland in the second game of a double-header. Smith would throw a second no-hitter on June 11, beating San Antonio 1–0, and he finished the year with seventeen victories between Double-A and Triple-A.

2002: Wichita completes an odd three-game rout of Round Rock, winning 13–6 after winning 13–1 and 13–2 the previous two days.

TWICE CHARMED

Just four pitchers have thrown two no-hitters in one Texas League season: George Hinrickson of Galveston in 1910, Dode Criss of Houston in 1915,

Larry Maxie of Austin in 1961 and Robert "Bud" Smith of Arkansas in 2000. Smith went 12-1 and was promoted to Triple-A in 2000.

MAY 7

1906: Greenville's Frank Moore throws a no-hitter against Cleburne, winning 1–0. Shortstop Baldy Louden scored the only run of the game, coming in from third base on a passed ball.

1932: Shreveport pitcher Milt Steengrafe hits four batters in a game with San Antonio. Steengrafe won ninety-five games in eight seasons in the league, including twenty-two in 1928, and served as an umpire in the league for fifteen years.

1963: San Antonio's forty-three-year-old first baseman, Bob Boyd, hits a go-ahead, two-run homer in the ninth to complete the cycle and give the Bullets a 10–9 victory at Amarillo. Boyd, who had broken into pro baseball with the Negro League's Memphis Red Sox in 1947, hit a combined .294 for the Houston Colts' Double-A and Triple-A affiliates in 1963.

1970: Dallas–Fort Worth catcher Jim Kelly sets a forgettable league record with five passed balls during San Antonio's seven-run fourth inning.

1975: Lafayette pitcher Frank Riccelli strikes out 7, including 4 in the ninth inning, in a 6–1 victory over Alexandria. His third strike to Bobby Taylor got past catcher Joey Martin for a passed ball. Riccelli won fourteen games for the Drillers in 1975 and struck out 120 men.

1999: El Paso ties a sixteen-year-old league record when eleven consecutive batters reach base and score in the Diablos' eleven-run fifth inning. Designated hitter Garry Maddox tied a league mark with two doubles in the inning. El Paso wound up beating Wichita 13–1.

MAY 8

1898: In the last game before the league disbands because of the failures of several clubs, Galveston pitcher Charles McDonald holds San Antonio hitless in a five-inning, 15–1 rout shortened by rain.

1905: John Lower of Waco pitches one of the greatest games in Texas League history without earning a decision. After allowing a single to Lon Ury of Dallas in the first inning, Lower throws 14.1 innings of no-hit ball. The game ends after 15 in a scoreless tie.

1912: Waco third baseman Roy Akin pulls off an unassisted triple play on a squeeze bunt in the first inning against Houston. Ironically, Akin had lined into an unassisted triple play while playing in the Pacific Coast League.

1922: Beaumont's Willis B. "Cy" Morgan hurls a no-hitter against Shreveport, winning 4–0. Morgan won just two other games in 1922, his last year in baseball.

1968: A crowd of 1,200 gets more than it expected from a half-price ticket promotion at Shreveport's Bonneau Peters Field. Following a 5–4 loss to San Antonio, fans were unable to leave the ballpark because an unidentified vandal had locked all the exit gates.

1979: Midland batters strike out sixteen times, but the Cubs still beat San Antonio, 8–2. Dodgers starter Ted Power struck out eleven but gave up thirteen hits, including four by the Cubs' Jim Tracy.

San Antonio pitcher Ted Power struck out eleven but gave up thirteen hits in 1979 against Midland. *Texas League collection.*

2013: Tulsa's Jaron Shepherd scores from second on a strikeout

as the Drillers top Arkansas 6–5 in eleven innings. Shepherd singled and went to second on a walk in the bottom of the eleventh and then came home when Elvin Ramirez's third strike to Kent Matthes bounced away from catcher Jett Bandy.

MAY 9

1902: Paris commits a league-record fifteen errors in a nine-inning loss to Dallas. Shortstop Bert "Skinny" Adrian had five of them.

1909: Shreveport's Bob Harmon pitches a 6–0, no-hit game against the Galveston Sandcrabs. Within weeks, Harmon was purchased by the St. Louis Cardinals and immediately began a nine-year Major League career, highlighted by becoming a twenty-game winner in 1911.

Shreveport's Damon Minor blasted a grand slam in both games of a double-header against Wichita in 1998. *Texas League collection.*

1962: El Paso outfielder Jesus Alou starts a streak that sees him hit safely in forty-eight of forty-nine games, including twenty-five in a row. Alou, one of the famous trio of Dominican brothers, wound up hitting .343 for El Paso in 1962.

1970: Dallas–Fort Worth's Dyar Miller, formerly a weak-hitting catcher, pitches a seven-inning no-hitter against Amarillo. Miller helped himself at the plate, driving in three runs with a homer and a single in a 10–0 victory over the Giants. Miller won a career-high twelve games for the Spurs in 1970.

1998: Shreveport's Damon Minor hits two grand slams, one in each end of a double-header, against Wichita. Minor was four for seven for the day with nine RBIs.

MAY 10

1909: Dallas pitcher O.C. "Rube" Peters shuts out Oklahoma City with four hits—all of them by outfielder William McCormick.

1916: San Antonio manager Harry L. Stewart pitches a 2–0 no-hitter against Waco in the last season of a professional career that began in 1904.

1961: Austin sets a league record with just one assist in the field in a 2–1 victory over Rio Grande Valley. The sole assist came on a grounder hit to first baseman Tommie Aaron in the sixth inning.

1966: Dallas–Fort Worth first baseman Tom Hillary muffs a pop-up, never touches the ball again and yet is credited with an unassisted double play. With runners at first and third and one out, Hillary dropped a pop-up by Ed Pacheco, and the ball rolled away. But because the infield fly rule was in effect, Pacheco was out automatically. When he continued to run around the bases after being called out, he was ruled an illegal runner, and another out was credited to Hillary, retiring the side.

1970: Because of a shortage of pitchers, thirty-eight-year-old Dallas–Fort Worth manager Joe Altobelli activates himself and works two innings in a 10–3 loss to Amarillo.

1999: The Arkansas Travelers score nine runs in the bottom of the ninth to beat El Paso 9–8. The outburst ends a string of twenty scoreless innings for Arkansas.

MAY 11

1917: Bob Couchman pitches a seven-inning no-hitter to lead Galveston to a 1–0 decision and double-header sweep at Fort Worth. Couchman drove in the only run of the game with a triple in the third inning. The victory was one of just two Couchman picked up for the Pirates in 1917.

1923: San Antonio's Ike Boone hits for the cycle as the Bears whip Dallas 21–4. Boone would go on to hit .402, still a modern-era league record.

1930: Wichita Falls slugger Larry Bettencourt goes five for five with a double and a home run as the Spudders whip Waco 13–9 in the opening game

San Antonio's Ike Boone, the last player to hit .400 in a Texas League season. *Courtesy Baseball Hall of Fame Library.*

of a double-header. Wichita Falls had sixteen hits in the game. The Spudders had sixteen more hits in the second contest, at least one by every player in the lineup—except Bettencourt, who was hitless.

1947: Harold "Hal" Epps of Houston sets a league record by tripling in his fifth straight game. Epps wound up leading the league in triples for the third time, and he holds the league career record with 112.

1949: Dallas second baseman Blas Monaco begins a streak of thirteen consecutive times on base in four games—with just two hits. He doubled and walked in his last two appearances on May 11. He got a hit as a pinch hitter on May 12. On May 13, he singled, was hit by a pitch and walked three times. The next day, he walked in his first at-bat and then was retired on a fly ball.

Harold "Hal" Epps holds the league record for career triples. *Texas League collection.*

1955: Mel Held of San Antonio is credited with a five-inning no-hitter when the first game of a double-header against Fort Worth is rained out with no score. His opponent, the Cats' Mike Lemish, gave up just a first-inning double to Dave Roberts.

1975: Nineteen-year-old San Antonio pitcher Tom McGough fires a 1–0 no-hitter against Shreveport. McGough walked just one and struck out eight. McGough went 2-2 in seven starts for San Antonio in 1975 before being promoted to Triple-A Oklahoma City.

1977: By being late to the ballpark, Arkansas pitcher Victor Cruz saves his spot on the roster. Cruz was supposed to be on a 5:00 p.m. flight to Class A in Florida, but when he arrived late at the ballpark, he did not have enough time to reach the airport. So Travelers manager Buzzy Keller started him instead, and Cruz responded with a four-hit, eleven-inning victory over Tulsa. The parent St. Louis Cardinals decided to keep Cruz in Arkansas.

2012: Four Northwest Arkansas pitchers combine on a no-hitter as the Naturals beat Springfield 2–0. Greg Holland, on a Major League rehab assignment, started and pitched a perfect first inning. Chris Dwyer, Brendan Lafferty and Kendal Volz followed, allowing just four runners.

2013: Northwest Arkansas' Juan Graterol hits a two-run homer in the top of the twentieth inning, and the Naturals hang on for a 5–4 victory in the longest game in Springfield's Texas League history.

MAY 12

1908: A mysterious woman leaves a small child with Houston pitcher W.E. Hester while the team's train is at the station in Hillsboro—and never returns. Only a hatbox with a note, the child's name and some details about the eighteen-year-old mother were found as clues. Houston manager Claude Reilly took up collections for the boy, Edmond Winters, as the team traveled around the league, and the "ward of the team" wound up at the Houston home of catcher Henry Dawson and his wife.

1951: Rex Barney, recently assigned to Fort Worth by Brooklyn to work on his control, walks sixteen in 7.2 innings in a 6–2 loss to Houston. In five outings for Fort Worth, Barney would last only 14 innings, walking thirty-nine, hitting four batters and making three wild pitches. The sixteen walks in a game remain a league record. Barney never returned to the Majors.

2002: Released a week earlier by the Toronto organization, Arkansas' Kenny James states his case for a second chance by driving in seven runs in a 14–6 victory over Tulsa. James hit .268 for the Travelers in '02 and .284 in '03 and then retired.

MAY 13

1903: Paris left fielder Clyde "Sis" Bateman delivers four home runs and a triple in a 13–7 romp at Corsicana. The Parisites' twenty-four hits convinced Corsicana's management to move the left-field wall back before the next home game.

1932: For the first time in the twentieth century, league owners vote to lower ticket prices, hoping to boost attendance in the Depression-ridden region.

1964: El Paso's Neil Martin establishes a league record by drawing a walk in his sixteenth consecutive game. He drew twenty-four walks during the streak, which began April 24. For the season, his last in baseball, Martin wound up with twenty-seven walks in twenty-five games.

1967: Felipe Leal tosses the first no-hitter in El Paso, beating Albuquerque 8–0. Leal, who had been the Rookie of the Year in the Mexican League, faced the minimum twenty-seven batters, as all three men to reach base were erased by double plays.

1972: Arkansas' Bob Forsch comes within a hit batsman of a perfect game, stopping Memphis 4–0 with a no-hitter in the seven-inning second game of a double-header. Forsch would go on to pitch in the Major Leagues from 1974 to 1989, winning 168 games.

2002: Arkansas' Hatuey Mendoza throws the first no-hitter at twenty-two-year-old Drillers Stadium, blanking Tulsa 3–0. The gem was one of the few highlights for the Dominican in 2002, as he went 3-10 with a 5.58 ERA for the Travelers and was released before the end of the season.

2013: Corpus Christi's Michael Burgess drives in a team-record eight runs in a 13–3 rout of San Antonio. Burgess had two three-run homers and a two-run double to match his season RBI total entering the game.

Bob Forsch came within one batter of a perfect game for Arkansas in 1972. *Texas League collection.*

MAY 14

1892: Galveston blasts Houston 20–0, with every batter in the lineup collecting at least one hit. Houston's only rally was snuffed by a triple play in the fifth, when left fielder Al McFarland made a diving catch and then threw to second to catch one runner. A relay to first ended the inning.

1923: San Antonio's W. Guy Morrison strikes out a league-record five times in a row in a game against Fort Worth. Exactly forty-three years later, Albuquerque outfielder Willie Crawford tied the mark in a loss to Dallas–Fort Worth.

1932: Galveston's Hank Thormahlen tosses a rain-shortened no-hitter, beating the recently relocated Tyler club 3–0. The no-hitter was the shortest in league history, as rain stopped the game in the bottom of the fifth.

1932: Fort Worth pitcher/manager Dick McCabe, one of the fastest workers in baseball, needs only sixty-three minutes to subdue Houston 1–0. McCabe and Houston's George Payne both threw five-hitters. McCabe, thirty-seven, won fifteen games in 1932.

1933: Beaumont's Joe Sullivan and Raymond Fritz combine to walk nine men—and also post the first combined no-hitter in league history, beating Dallas 6–3.

1939: In one of the wildest extra-innings games in league history, Fort Worth edges Houston 11–10 in thirteen innings. The game was tied 3–3 through nine innings, and then both teams scored four runs in the eleventh. Houston went up 10–7 in the top of the thirteenth, but then Fort Worth rallied for four runs in the bottom of the inning.

May 15

1947: Dallas's Bobby Hogue pitches a one-hitter and goes three for three at the plate as the Rebels top Houston 5–0. Hogue went on to win sixteen games for Dallas and post a 2.31 ERA in 1947.

1949: A fire of undetermined origin destroys 75 percent of LaGrave Field in Fort Worth. The Cats played as scheduled the next day, beating San Antonio 2–0 in front of almost four thousand fans and remnants of the Fort Worth Fire Department, which continued to pour water on the smoldering grandstands.

1950: Three Shreveport runners score on a strikeout in a game with Oklahoma City, thanks to a passed ball and a wild throw.

1973: El Paso hitters strike out seventeen times in twelve innings and still manage to beat Alexandria 6–5.

2006: Frisco pitchers strike out seventeen San Antonio batters in a 5–3 victory. Starter John Danks whiffed twelve in the first 6 innings alone. Danks struck out eighty-two in just 69.1 innings for the RoughRiders in 2006.

May 16

1889: Dallas's Pete Daniels has an up-and-down day in a twelve-inning game against Austin that winds up in a 15–15 tie. Normally a pitcher, Daniels started the game at third base because of injuries on the club. He had five hits but was charged with seven errors; he pitched the final five innings of the game, giving up no runs and two hits.

1896: Umpire Ed Clark ejects the groundskeeper for brushing off the plate without his permission during a sixteen-inning, 5–5 tie between Paris and Waco.

1903: Arthur "Rip" Ragan of Dallas pitches a 1–0 no-hitter against Paris, allowing just one ball to be hit out of the infield and one base runner, on a ninth-inning walk. Ragan went on to win twenty-five games for the Giants in 1903, his only season in the league.

1918: Fort Worth's Paul Wachtel, one of the league's greatest pitchers, hurls a 2–0 no-hitter against Dallas in his first season in the Texas League.

1939: Shreveport's Jim Bivin leads the Sports to a 16–2 laugher against Fort Worth, holding the Cats to three hits and driving in six runs with a bases-loaded single and a grand slam.

1969: The El Paso pitching staff begins a string of fifty-three consecutive scoreless innings, which includes five consecutive shutouts. The shutouts tied a record set by Austin in 1907, while the fifty-three scoreless innings broke the existing record.

2002: Midland's Jacques Landry completes back-to-back monster games with a seven-RBI night against El Paso on the strength of a single and two homers. On May 15, Landry had two doubles and two home runs. The right-hander drove in twenty-seven runs in thirty games before a promotion to Triple-A.

2005: In front of a packed house—most of whom were schoolchildren—at Arkansas' Ray Winder Field, Tulsa's Ryan Spilborghs hits for the cycle in a 5–2 victory. He had a two-run triple in the first, a single in the third, a two-run homer in the fifth and a double in the seventh. Spilborghs hit .341 in seventy-one games for the Drillers in 2005 and had fifty-four RBIs.

MAY 17

1933: Jake Atz resigns as a Texas League umpire to return as manager of the Fort Worth Cats—a job he had held from 1914 to 1929.

1968: Roy Foster of Memphis raises his batting average from .167 to .259 in one night, going six for six to lead the Blues to a 15–10 victory over Albuquerque. Foster wound up at .270 for the season.

1973: Arkansas' John Denny throws his first no-hitter as a professional, stopping Midland 8–1. The Cubs scored in the fourth on a walk and two errors. Denny went on to pitch parts of thirteen seasons in the Major Leagues, and he led the National League in victories in 1983, when he went 19-6 for the Phillies.

1974: Victoria right-hander Jackson Todd hurls a 3–0 no-hitter against Arkansas. Todd, who had been winless in his three previous starts, allowed only five runners, four via walks and one on an error. The right-hander went 11-8 and struck out 115 in 173 innings for the Toros.

1976: El Paso ties a league record with five home runs in the first inning of a 10–4 romp over Arkansas. With one out, Fred Frazier, Steve Strother and Willie Aikens homered consecutively. The next batter, Tom Donahue, doubled, and then Lawrence Rush homered. After a double and a strikeout, Joe Zagarino hit homer number five.

1987: Jackson's Gregg Jefferies hits for the cycle, but the nineteen-year-old's efforts aren't enough as the Mets fall to El Paso 12–10. It was part of a big season for the former number-one draft pick, who hit .367 with twenty homers and forty-eight doubles and drove in 101 runs.

2007: Springfield's Juan Lucena goes five for five after entering the game as a pinch hitter in the second inning. He also tied the game at seven with a sacrifice fly in the seventh inning.

MAY 18

1924: Fort Worth begins a five-game winning streak in which the games take an average of fewer than ninety minutes each. Fort Worth pitchers gave up just twenty-three hits and twelve walks during the games.

1925: Fort Worth's Ziggy Sears collected three homers, a double and a postwar high of eleven RBIs as his Cats drub San Antonio 19–8. Sears's RBI total was topped only by Jay Clarke's sixteen in 1902 and Bill Kemmer's twelve in 1898.

Fort Worth's Ziggy Sears drove in eleven runs in a 19–8 victory over San Antonio in 1925. *Texas League collection.*

1932: Texas League owners decide to move the Wichita Falls club to Longview to take advantage of oilfield activity and a booming local economy. The next day, the former Wichita Falls club is pounded 17–2 in Beaumont.

1966: Johnny Kindl caps a three-game, ten-for-fourteen hitting outburst against El Paso with a five-for-five performance in Arkansas' 9–5 victory. Kindl, who had been hitting .130 in six previous games with the Travs, collected three singles and two homers while driving in four runs.

1971: Two Amarillo pitchers strike out fifteen Arkansas batters in the Giants' 3–2, eleven-inning victory. Greg Ryerson fanned twelve in eight innings, and Dave Hernandez, who worked the final three innings, struck out three more. Amarillo won the game when Arkansas' Rudy Arroyo, who struck out six, walked in the winning run.

1994: Ty Boykin blasts a grand slam in the bottom of the ninth inning to give Midland a 10–6 decision over Arkansas. It was one of just five homers Boykin hit in 1994.

1996: Two long hitting streaks end in a double-header between Arkansas and El Paso. The Diablos' Ronnie Belliard had his twenty-three-game streak snapped in the first game, and the Travelers' Keith Johns had his end at nineteen in the second game. Belliard went on to play parts of thirteen seasons in the big leagues and appeared in the 2004 All-Star Game. Johns hit just .246 in 1994 and appeared in just two games in the Majors, for the Boston Red Sox in 1998.

1997: Texas League teams score a record ninety-three runs in one day. The scores of the four games were: San Antonio 22, Tulsa 12; El Paso 12, Jackson 10; Midland 12, Arkansas 8; and Shreveport 10, Wichita 7. As part of the big hitting night, San Antonio's Jay Kirkpatrick stroked a single and two home runs, collecting eight RBIs.

2013: Midland's Anthony Aliotti goes four for five with three homers and a double, driving in eight runs in the RockHounds' 12–4 victory over Corpus Christi.

May 19

1958: Dallas explodes for seven runs in the tenth inning to beat Corpus Christi 13–6. Art Dunham led the Rangers with two triples, a double and a single in six times at bat, good for five RBIs. Dunham got three of his RBIs in the tenth with a bases-loaded triple.

1963: Nineteen-year-old Jose Cardenal hits two homers in El Paso's 18–3 romp over San Antonio, giving him thirteen since he arrived in the league on April 29. The Cuban finished the season with thirty-six homers in 125 games.

1969: Bobby Grich leads a seventeen-hit Dallas–Fort Worth offense, going five for five in the Spurs' 13–11 victory over Albuquerque. He collected hits off of four different Dodgers pitchers. Grich began a seventeen-year career in the Major Leagues the next season, a career that included six appearances in the All-Star Game.

1972: Arkansas' Al Hrabosky strikes out sixteen El Paso batters en route to a three-hit, 3–1 victory. Hrabosky, later dubbed the "Mad Hungarian," went on to pitch in the Majors for thirteen seasons and had a stellar 1975 season, going 13-3 with a league-high twenty-two saves.

1979: Four Midland pitchers issue fifteen walks, with ten of them resulting in runs, as Arkansas clobbers the Cubs 20–5. Cubs starter Lee Smith had eight of the free passes in just three innings. The Travs' Randy Thomas was chief beneficiary of the wild Midland pitching, walking five times and scoring five runs.

2003: Round Rock scores nine runs in the top of the ninth inning, rallying to beat Midland 12–8. Express shortstop Tommy Whiteman had two homers in the inning, a two-run shot in his first time to the plate and a three-run blast the second time.

MAY 20

1892: Houston's Ollie Pickering has seven singles in seven consecutive at-bats to lead his club to a 20–10 victory over Fort Worth. The season was the first in baseball for Pickering, who would play in the minors on and off until 1922, when he was fifty-two years old.

1918: Shreveport's Jack Enright walks seven, hits a batter, delivers a wild pitch and gives up twelve runs in the first inning of what turns into a 24–4 loss to San Antonio. Gassers manager Mike O'Neill came in from left field to finish the game, giving up eleven more runs on fourteen hits.

1925: Fort Worth wraps up a three-game pounding of San Antonio with a 24–12 rout that ended with players serving as umpires after San Antonio fans stormed the field. For the series, Panthers left fielder Ziggy Sears had six home runs, sixteen RBIs, twelve runs and fourteen hits in eighteen at-bats.

1952: Longtime Texas League president Tom Kayser is born in Hinsdale, Illinois.

1956: Fort Worth abuses San Antonio pitching for the second night in a row, pounding twenty hits in a 17–4 victory over the Missions. On May 19, the Cats had rallied from an 11–2 deficit for a 16–12 victory, led by a five-for-five night from leadoff man Dick Gray.

1966: Tom Hutton hits for the cycle, pacing Albuquerque to a 16–6 thrashing of El Paso. Hutton was five for five with six RBIs. Hutton hit .340 and drove in eighty-one runs for the Dodgers in 103 games in 1966, earning a promotion to Triple-A.

1974: Frank Snook of Alexandria throws a no-hitter against Victoria in the first game of a double-header, allowing just a sixth-inning walk to designated hitter Terry Senn. Snook made just four starts for the Aces in 1974 before being sent to Triple-A.

2001: Midland defeats Round Rock 15–11 in a game that sees a record-tying seventeen doubles. In fact, all but two of the batters in the game had at least one extra-base hit.

2003: Tulsa turns a triple play in the top of the ninth to snuff a Frisco rally and then gets a homer from Brad Hawpe in the tenth for a 2–1 victory. Hawpe reached the Major Leagues the next season and was named to the All-Star Game in 2009.

2006: Springfield scores eight runs after two outs in the top of the ninth inning, rallying to shock Arkansas 11–10.

John Van Cuyk led the league in strikeouts in 1946. *Texas League collection.*

May 21

1935: In spite of ten walks in 7.1 innings, Tulsa's Art McDougall beats Fort Worth 6–4. The Cats left sixteen men on base.

1946: John Van Cuyk of Fort Worth strikes out 19 in defeating Houston 4–2. He went on to lead the league with 206 but had just one more season with more than 100 strikeouts after that.

MAY

1947: Beaumont's Jack McKinney faces only twenty-eight Shreveport batters in a 6–0 no-hitter. The nine-inning contest was played in just one hour and twenty-nine minutes. McKinney won a career-best thirteen games in 1947.

1955: Beaumont is shut out for the fourth game in a row and extends its streak of scoreless innings to forty-three. Three of the Exporters' losses, though, were 1–0 scores.

1957: Austin's Paul Rambone homers in his first three times at bat to help the Senators to a 13–4 victory in the second game of a double-header against Fort Worth. Rambone had sixteen more home runs during the rest of the season but hit just .238.

1964: Hours after pitching a three-hit, 1–0, ten-inning win over Fort Worth, Austin pitcher Jerry Hummitzsch is killed in a one-car accident in Austin. Teammate Walt Hriniak, a passenger in the car, survived but suffered head and chest injuries. Hummitzsch had thrown a no-hitter for Austin the previous season.

1964: Albuquerque's Braxton Bailey scores the only run of the game with an inside-the-park home run against San Antonio. Bailey went on to the best year of his baseball career, hitting nineteen homers and driving in one hundred runs with a .321 average.

1972: Jackie Stripling throws the second no-hitter for Arkansas in eight days, beating Midland 3–1. Stripling walked seven and also had a wild pitch.

1987: Shreveport relief pitcher Stu Tate collects his first hit in two years in the top of the twenty-first inning to launch a rally and give the Captains a 4–3 victory at San Antonio. The game, which took six hours and four minutes to complete, saw five Shreveport pitchers throw shutout ball for the last thirteen innings.

MAY 22

1935: Fort Worth pitcher Keith Frazier walks eleven yet still beats Tulsa 3–2. Frazier wound up the 1935 season with ninety-four walks in 166 innings for the Cats and Los Angeles in the Pacific Coast League.

Pam Postema, who broke the professional baseball umpires' gender barrier, makes a call during the 1981 season. *Texas League collection.*

1945: Jake Atz, who led the Fort Worth Panthers to six pennants from 1920 to 1925, dies at the age of sixty-five in New Orleans.

1981: Umpire Pam Postema, making her first trip to El Paso, begins a series of eleven games in which she and her partner Larry Degate would eject thirteen managers, coaches and players.

1999: Shreveport, playing its 10,000th regular-season game as a member of the Texas League, beats Wichita 6–4.

2001: Five Tulsa pitchers combine for a league-record twenty-five strikeouts, and Shreveport's pitchers strike out eighteen more in a seventeen-inning game at Tulsa. Tulsa had just three hits—two of them by David Meliah, the only hitter in the game who didn't strike out.

2002: Wichita sets three league records in the big fourth inning of a 19–2 blowout against Tulsa. The Wranglers had sixteen consecutive batters reach base and fourteen consecutive runners score, a league high for a fourth inning. Their thirteen hits in the inning tied a record as well.

MAY 23

1888: San Antonio loses to Fort Worth 6–5 and then folds, ending the first incarnation of Texas League baseball in the Alamo City in 1888. The city got a team back on July 4 when the Austin club was moved to San Antonio.

1921: John P. "Bull" Henry, the Shreveport Gassers' regular catcher, throws out four base runners from right field. Henry, a former big-league catcher, had never played the outfield before.

1932: In the home debut of the newly located club, Longview's middle infield combo of shortstop Art Scharein and second baseman Ollie Bejma takes part in six double plays. More than six thousand fans turned out to watch the hometown club top Fort Worth 4–3.

1973: Frank George drives in seven runs with a grand slam and a three-run double to help El Paso hold off San Antonio 14–13. George's grand slam came in the ten-run third inning when the Sun Kings took an 11–2 lead, but El Paso didn't clinch the game until scoring three in the bottom of the ninth.

1999: San Antonio falls to Jackson 8–1 as Missions pitchers tie a league record with six hit batsmen. San Antonio starter Widd Workman is charged with five of them. (The league record was set by A.L. Gheen of Houston, who hit six Dallas batters on June 8, 1922.)

MAY 24

1897: Replacement umpire Dan LaHugh, summoned to the ballpark in Dallas after regular umpire John Brennan failed to show up, has a short assignment. Austin manager Pop Weikert refused to let his players take the field with the local umpire calling balls and strikes, so LaHugh had to forfeit the game to Dallas.

1934: San Antonio's Ash Hillin pitches 8.2 innings of shutout ball in relief as the Missions pound Tulsa 19–5. Hillin, who led the league with twenty-four victories in 1934, came into the game after the Oilers had scored all their runs.

San Antonio's Ash Hillin led the league with twenty-four victories in 1934. *Texas League collection.*

1954: Ray Cucchiarini is killed in a one-car accident on his way to Houston. The Buffs had just claimed the outfielder, who was hitting .341, on waivers from Fort Worth. He lost control of his car on wet pavement and hit a tree near the East Texas town of Huntsville.

1956: San Antonio third baseman Brooks Robinson rips a three-run homer in the bottom of the thirteenth to rally the Missions to a 12–9 victory over Fort Worth. Robinson played in parts of just four seasons in the minors before launching a twenty-three-year career with the Baltimore Orioles that saw him inducted into the National Baseball Hall of Fame.

1968: Bob Watkins of the Dallas–Fort Worth Spurs throws the first no-hitter by a Dallas pitcher in twenty-one years, leading his club past Memphis, 2–0. The next day, Luis Penalver threw a no-hitter for the Spurs in the first game of a double-header.

1991: Midland routs Jackson 12–1 despite getting just four hits. Jackson pitchers Kevin Coffman and Keith Kaiser walked eleven batters in the first two innings, when the Angels scored all their runs.

MAY 25

1940: Beaumont right-hander Virgil Trucks throws the third no-hitter of his career, a 1–0, seven-inning effort against Tulsa. "Fire" Trucks made it to the Majors the next year, launching a big-league career that lasted until 1958.

1961: Victoria fans find out their team is moving to Ardmore, Oklahoma, and then see the Rosebuds drop a double-header against Tulsa, 7–6 and 6–3, in front of 524 sad souls.

1961: Four days after losing at home in sixteen innings, Austin beats visiting Rio Grande Valley 7–6 in seventeen innings. The Senators also had played ten innings on May 21.

1988: A rainstorm ends the only scoreless extra-innings game in seventeen years of baseball in Midland. The Angels and Jackson were tied 0–0 when the storm arrived in the bottom of the tenth.

2000: Roy Oswalt, called up from Class A for one start at Round Rock, pitches a five-hit, 5–0 shutout of league-leading San Antonio. Oswalt struck out fifteen, the most in the league in almost twenty years, and wound up going 11-4 for the Express in 2000.

2000: El Paso's Alex Cabrera clubs a three-run homer in the first inning and adds a three-run shot in the ninth, but the Diablos still fall to Midland 11–10.

2008: San Antonio records the 7,000th victory in franchise history, topping Arkansas 5–2 in the city's 104th season in the league.

MAY 26

1895: Dallas drubs Houston 30–10 in a game called after seven innings to allow Houston to catch a train.

1914: Beaumont Oilers pitcher Grover Brant tosses his second career Texas League no-hitter, winning 7–0 over Galveston. Brant went on to win twenty-three games for the Oilers in 1914, the best season of his career.

1928: San Antonio center fielder Leo Najo sets a league record for outfielders with twelve putouts in one game. Najo, a native of Mexico whose real name was Leonardo Alanis, was a .321 hitter in twelve seasons in the minors.

1930: Beaumont's Oscar "Ox" Eckhardt, a .355 hitter in his three Texas League seasons, collects his tenth consecutive hit, the second-best streak in league history.

2002: El Paso's Luis Terrero hits for the cycle, goes five for five and drives in six runs, but his team still loses to Round Rock, 15–11. The Express's Henri Stanley was a homer short of the cycle, also going five for five.

2005: Rudy Gomez, who had played second base for the first eighteen innings of Wichita's game against Corpus Christi, is the winning pitcher when his teammates score five runs in the Wranglers' 7–2 victory. The losing pitcher was Eric Riggs, who had entered the game as a pinch hitter in the sixth and stayed in the lineup as the designated hitter. Riggs walked the bases loaded in the twentieth and then gave up two singles and a double.

2008: Midland first baseman Tommy Everidge drives in ten runs with three homers as the RockHounds drub Tulsa 17–6. Everidge went on to record a career-high 115 RBIs in 2008.

MAGIC NUMBER TWENTY

Since 1900, there have been just eight pitchers who have won twenty games in both the Majors and the Texas League. The first was Dickey Kerr,

Howie Pollet is the only pitcher to have multiple twenty-win seasons in the Texas League and the Majors. *Texas League collection.*

who was 21-10 for Fort Worth in 1915 and 21-9 for the Chicago White Sox in 1920. The next was Dizzy Dean, who was 26-10 for Houston in 1931 and then won twenty or more games four times for the St. Louis Cardinals. Howie Pollet of the Houston Buffs is the only one of the eight to have had two twenty-win seasons in the TL and two or more twenty-win seasons in the Majors.

MAY 27

1895: Houston releases infielder Joe Bouchers—so he can join the Texas League staff of umpires.

1909: Dallas catcher Jack Onslow scores on his own strikeout. Batting in the seventh inning, he swings and misses a curveball, which bounces to the top of the grandstand and lodges there. As the Fort Worth players try to figure out what to do, Onslow circles the bases.

1923: Houston shortstop Les Bell laces five straight doubles in the Buffs' 22–4 victory over Dallas. Bell finished the season with thirty-five doubles.

1959: Austin ties a league record with six triples in a 27–5 pasting of the Mexico City Tigers. In the club's first visit to the Mexican capital city, the Senators built a 27–0 lead through six and a half innings.

1964: El Paso's Dave Turnbull, after being called into the game in the second inning, retires twenty-three consecutive batters—every one he faced—in a 6–1 victory over Austin. Turnbull won eleven games for the Sun Kings in 1964.

1969: Arkansas' Reggie Cleveland celebrates the birth of a daughter by shutting out Shreveport 6–0, allowing the Braves just one hit. The twenty-one-year-old Canadian needed just eighty-six pitches to complete the one-hour-and-forty-minute game.

1981: For the first time in league history, a woman serves as a manager. Christina Stemp won the "Manager for a Night" contest sponsored by the *San Antonio Light* newspaper, but she didn't have many tough decisions to make—the Dodgers trailed 9–0 after an inning and a half, on the way to a 12–1 loss to Arkansas.

MAY 28

1949: Dallas records an unusual triple play in a 9–4 victory over Tulsa. With men at first and second, Dallas center fielder Ben Guintini caught a ball with his back to the fence and fired it back to the infield to double off the runner at first. First baseman Jerry Witte then threw to second base, where the umpire called out the runner Booby Carson for leaving the base too soon.

1955: Fort Worth catcher Joe Pignatano accidentally goes to the plate in the seventh spot in the batting order, instead of Maury Wills, and hits a home run that is nullified on appeal from the Shreveport dugout. Willis is called out, and then Pignatano, batting in his proper eighth spot, hits another homer to almost the same spot as his nullified one.

1963: Apparently upset by bench jockeying, El Paso's Jose Cardenal rushes the Austin dugout, brandishing what in various reports was either a knife or a blunt instrument. Teammate Julio Linares disarmed the outfielder, who was not ejected from the game. (The league placed Cardenal on probation on June 3.)

Julio Linares helped defuse an incident involving El Paso teammate Jose Cardenal. *Texas League collection.*

1980: Midland's Henry Mack strikes out sixteen before being ejected from the game in the eighth inning. Mack is tossed after bumping the home-plate umpire during an argument.

2010: Arkansas pitchers walk fourteen San Antonio batters, including a record-tying seven in the seventh inning, in a 16–4 loss to the Missions.

MAY 29

1890: William Stockamp, who played third base for Waco under the name of Mussey, dies after a brief illness at a boardinghouse. Houston and Waco played two benefit games to help defray burial costs for Stockamp, with the second game becoming necessary after receipts from the first game were stolen.

1912: Umpire Mike Jacobs, needing to catch a train to his next assignment, departs the field with Dallas and Beaumont tied at eight after eight innings. After twenty minutes of discussion, a player from each team was appointed to call the game. The teams played one more scoreless inning, called it a tie and left immediately—also to catch their trains.

1947: Houston and Shreveport play to an eighteen-inning scoreless tie, the longest such game in league history. The game ended at the 10:30 p.m. curfew.

1956: Austin wins three games in one day, beating Oklahoma City in eighteen innings in a game that ends after midnight and then sweeping a double-header from the Indians later in the day.

1958: At the age of fifty-four, Tulsa coach Pepper Martin puts himself into a game as a pinch runner. The "Wild Horse of the Osage" was stranded at second base in his last appearance as a player.

2007: Springfield's Colby Rasmus drives in seven runs with two doubles and a home run as the Cardinals outslug San Antonio 12–11. Rasmus, the Cardinals' number-one draft pick in 2005, debuted in the Major Leagues two years later.

MAY 30

1912: Grover Brant of the Beaumont Oilers strikes out fourteen and walks five in a 2–1, twelve-inning no-hitter against Fort Worth. Brant was just 7-9 for the Oilers in 1912 but won 23 games in 1914.

1939: Fort Worth relief pitcher Ray Starr throws the final 18.2 innings of a 20-inning victory over Oklahoma City. Starr, who had just joined the Cats, allowed no runs and seven hits. Starr won 18 games for the Cats in 1939 and 214 overall in the minors.

1963: Tulsa outlasts Albuquerque 9–8 in seventeen innings in the longest game in league history: five hours and forty-seven minutes. Jim Beauchamp drove in six runs with a home run, a double and two singles in seven at-bats.

2007: San Antonio leadoff hitter Will Venable hits for the cycle as the Missions top Springfield 6–3. Venable's day included a three-run homer and a double in the ninth. The son of former big-leaguer Max Venable joined the parent San Diego Padres the next season.

MAY 31

1908: San Antonio pitcher Fred (Winchell) Cook throws a no-hitter for eleven innings but winds up losing to Waco 2–0 in the thirteenth.

1915: Eddie Donalds of Waco hurls an 11–0 no-hit victory over Shreveport. The only two base runners against Donalds reached via errors. Donalds had at least ten victories in every season he pitched in the minors (1911–23) and won a league-high thirty games in 1914.

1966: Moose Stubing, benched before the game because of a .165 batting average, hits two home runs as a pinch hitter and defensive replacement, including the game-winner in the eleventh inning of Arkansas' 5–4 victory over Dallas–Fort Worth.

2000: Tulsa's Ryan Lane steals home in the bottom of the twelfth to give the Drillers a 4–3 victory over Shreveport. It was one of just fifteen steals for Lane in 2000.

2000: El Paso's Alex Cabrera hits his league-record twenty-first homer of the month and brings his one-month RBI total to an even fifty.

2001: San Antonio's Craig Kuzmic drives in seven runs as the Missions bury El Paso 21–4. Kuzmic had a three-run homer in the first, an RBI double in the second, an RBI single in the fourth and a two-RBI double in the sixth.

2006: Despite getting just one hit, San Antonio tops Tulsa 2–1. The Missions scored on an error, their only hit (a ground-rule double by Oswaldo Navarro) and a groundout. They scored the eventual game-winner in the sixth with a three-base error and a sacrifice fly by Sebastien Boucher. Tulsa starter Steve Register got the loss despite allowing just one hit and one walk in eight innings.

WELCOME BACK

El Paso first baseman Alex Cabrera, who had not played in the United States since 1996, returned in a big way in 2000. In May, the twenty-eight-year-old Venezuelan hit .394 with twenty-one home runs (second most in pro baseball) and drove in fifty runs. He had a home run in six consecutive games from May 9 to May 14, including a stretch of five homers in six consecutive at-bats. In eighty-two minor-league games, he hit .353 with

Alex Cabrera returned to baseball with a splash in 2000. *Photo by Tom Kayser.*

thirty-nine homers and ninety-four RBIs, and on June 25, he was promoted to the Arizona Diamondbacks.

June

June 1

1915: After being ejected in the eighth inning, Galveston manager Paul Sentell gets into a fistfight with umpire George Miller. They continued to brawl even after police arrived, and both wound up arrested and charged with fighting in public.

1935: Charlie Engel and Sam Harshaney both deliver their first hits of the game in the bottom of the twenty-first inning, giving San Antonio a 4–3 victory over Dallas.

1940: Oklahoma City's Charlie Fuchs throws his second seven-inning no-hitter in as many years but doesn't realize it until after the game. A dribbler back to Fuchs from San Antonio's Pete Kraus was originally ruled a hit, but the official scorer changed his ruling to an error on Fuchs after questioning players from both teams after the game.

1955: Dallas Eagles owner Dick Burnett, a flamboyant East Texas oilman who integrated the Texas League and attracted the largest one-day crowd in league history, dies of a heart attack.

1960: Rio Grande Valley scores seven runs in the top of the ninth and then holds off a five-run rally in the bottom of the inning to edge

Amarillo 18–17. The Giants' Chuck Hiller went six for six, and each team totaled twenty hits.

1962: The largest crowd to see a minor-league game in San Antonio pours into Mission Stadium and is rewarded with a 4–3 victory over El Paso. The 12,946 fans saw the Sun Kings' Carl Boles go four for four with a single, two doubles and a home run but get just one RBI.

1963: San Antonio pitchers stifle El Paso's hitters in both ends of a double-header. Cliff Davis threw a no-hitter against the Sun Kings in the first game, and Joe Hoerner allowed just two hits in a 1–0 shutout in the nightcap. (Five Texas League games were shutouts on the same night, as Austin blanked Amarillo and Albuquerque and Tulsa split a double-header.)

1974: San Antonio's Larry Anderson throws the third no-hitter in the league in a sixteen-day span, beating Victoria 6–0. Jackson Todd, who had thrown the first of the three no-hitters, was serving as the Toros' manager at the end of the game after manager Joe Frazier's ejection in the fourth.

1983: On one of the better nights of his playing career, Jackson's Billy Beane goes four for six and drives in four runs as the Mets top Tulsa 12–11 in ten innings. Beane went on to much greater success as an executive, leading the Oakland Athletics.

Fernando Valenzuela pitched a two-hitter for Midland against Arkansas in 1991 as he was working his way back to the Major Leagues. *Texas League collection.*

1991: Former Cy Young Award winner Fernando Valenzuela,

attempting to return to the Major Leagues after his release by Los Angeles, tosses a complete-game two-hitter as Midland tops Arkansas 2–0 in front of 12,246 fans in Little Rock.

JUNE 2

1906: Cleburne breaks up a scoreless tie with a five-run fourteenth inning in a duel in Waco. Navigators pitcher Frank Browning allowed just two hits in the first thirteen innings but then committed two errors in the Railroaders' big inning. Rick Adams gave up two hits, walked one and struck out fifteen for Cleburne.

1909: The Drucke brothers, both sports stars at TCU, make a memorable debut with Dallas. Louis Drucke, throwing to his brother Oscar Drucke, struck out fourteen and won 4–0. Oscar went one for two at the plate and scored a run. Louis went on to go 14-4 in 1909, and he finished the season with the New York Giants. Oscar played just two more seasons, both in the minors.

1922: A carelessly dropped cigarette starts a blaze that interrupts Shreveport's game at Wichita Falls and results in major damage to the ballpark and the destruction of more than sixty cars. With temporary seating in place, the teams played in front of more than 2,400 fans the next day.

1974: Shreveport sweeps a double-header from El Paso, 13–8 and 13–12, getting thirteen hits in each game.

1977: Milt Steengrafe, who pitched eight seasons in the league and is its longest-serving umpire (fifteen seasons), dies at the age of seventy-nine in Oklahoma City. He called balls and strikes from 1938 to 1942 and from 1946 to 1955.

2013: Corpus Christi's George Springer drives in five of the Hooks' ten runs in the first inning of a 13–9 victory over Arkansas. Springer laced a two-run double his first time up in the inning and then finished it off with a three-run homer.

JUNE 3

1896: San Antonio rallies from an 18–10 deficit with four runs in the eighth inning and five more in the ninth to knock off Austin 19–18. The teams combined for thirty-six hits, including eleven triples.

1946: Former big-leaguer Henry "Prince" Oana of Dallas finishes the first month of his season at 7-0 with a 0.56 ERA. The thirty-eight-year-old would play five more seasons as a pro, with 262 home runs and eighty-three pitching victories.

Henry "Prince" Oana was a threat both as a pitcher and a hitter for Dallas. *Texas League collection.*

1960: Amarillo right-hander Jerry Neal allows thirteen hits and eleven runs in seven innings—and still gets a win in the Gold Sox's 12–11 decision over Austin. Denny Lemaster pitched a complete game for Austin, giving up thirteen hits and walking nine. He gave up eleven of Amarillo's runs in the first two innings.

1965: Austin's Vince Ferguson has four hits and five RBIs, including the game-winner in a four-run ninth inning, as the Braves top Albuquerque 11–10.

1977: El Paso scores twelve runs in the final two innings but comes up one short in a 19–18 loss to Tulsa.

1983: Tulsa's Mike Rubel pounds Jackson for a triple and two home runs, driving in seven runs in a 10–2 rout. Rubel hit .302 and drove in sixty-one runs in seventy-two games for the Drillers before he was promoted to Triple-A.

1992: El Paso catcher Bob Kappesser hits his first professional home run in his 600th Texas League at-bat as the Diablos beat Wichita 6–5. Kappesser played seven seasons in the minors and hit just three more homers.

2000: Round Rock third baseman Morgan Ensberg hits three home runs and drives in eight runs in the Express's 12–9 victory over Shreveport. His last homer, a three-run shot, gave Round Rock the lead in the top of the ninth. Ensberg hit twenty homers and drove in ninety-eight runs for the Express in 2000 while hitting .300.

2011: San Antonio tops Arkansas in its final at-bat for the third night in a row, this time rallying from a two-run deficit to win 6–5.

Morgan Ensberg blasted three homers and drove in eight runs for Round Rock on June 3, 2000. *Photo by Tom Kayser.*

JUNE 4

1929: San Antonio scores eleven runs in the seventh inning and winds up edging Beaumont 13–11. Three San Antonio hitters had two hits in the big inning: Harvey Ballew, Lymon Nason and Jim Riley.

1931: San Antonio's Euel Moore, the only member of the Chickasaw Nation to play in the Major Leagues, throws a no-hitter to beat Galveston 3–0. Moore pitched for parts of three seasons in the National League, appearing in sixty-one games.

1939: Texas League umpire (and former pitching star) Joe Pate misses his first inning in almost seven years when he is struck on the kneecap by a foul tip during a game in Houston.

1997: Midland scores six times in the top of the ninth and then holds on for a 17–14 victory at El Paso. Kevin Young had a double, two homers and five RBIs for the Angels, who gave up six runs in the bottom of the ninth.

JUNE 5

1911: Dallas manager Curley Maloney pieces together a lineup from eleven pitchers and utility players after most of his regulars miss the train from Waco to Dallas. Not surprisingly, the makeshift club fell to Oklahoma City 21–6.

1923: San Antonio introduces new uniforms that, for the first time, include numbers.

1930: Wichita Falls sets a league record with seven double plays in a 6–1 victory over Waco. Second baseman Linn Storti takes part in five of them.

1952: Fort Worth pitcher Elroy Face pitches nine no-hit innings against Houston and then gives up a hit in the tenth moments after his team had scored three runs. After Ed Merkowski singled to lead off the bottom of the tenth, Face retired the side to finish with a one-hitter.

1961: Victoria regains a place in the Texas League when it is announced that the Rio Grande Valley Giants will transfer the rest of their games to Victoria beginning June 10. Victoria fans had lost their team to Ardmore, Oklahoma, on May 26.

1962: Tulsa shortstop Daryl Robertson has a busy and successful day. Traded to the organization during the day, he joined the Oilers in time for their game at San Antonio. His error in the third inning led to three unearned runs, but then he drove in the go-ahead run in the fourteenth with an opposite-field single.

1968: San Antonio's Dean Burk fires a 1–0 no-hitter against Albuquerque. The losing pitcher was Dick Armstrong, who had thrown a no-hitter against Dallas–Fort Worth on May 2.

1977: Tulsa and El Paso follow a 19–18 slugfest with another one. Tulsa made it two for two in big-scoring games with a 16–14 decision, fed by a four-for-five night by Billy Sample.

1996: San Antonio wins its tenth game in a row, topping El Paso 12–0 behind a five-hitter by Eric Weaver.

2000: Backup catcher David Ross drives in six runs with a grand slam and a two-run homer, leading San Antonio over Arkansas, 13–2. Ross made his big-league debut two years later and through 2013 had appeared in 694 games for six teams.

2001: Juan Silvestre's single in the tenth inning gives San Antonio an 11–10 victory over Shreveport. The Missions had tied the game in the bottom of the eighth, moments after the Swamp Dragons had scored eight times in the top of the inning.

2001: Round Rock's Jason Lane drives in eight runs with three doubles and a homer in a 14–5 victory at Arkansas. It was part of a monster season for Lane, as he hit .316 with thirty-eight homers, thirty-six doubles and 124 RBIs for the Express.

2007: Corpus Christi collects a club-record six homers in a 9–4 victory at Midland, including two by Noochie Varner. Varner, a minor-league veteran, finished his career in 2007, hitting .287 with six home runs for the Hooks in ninety-eight games.

DOUBLE THREAT

Cy Forsythe, whose batting average topped .300 in 1911–12 for Dallas, started his baseball career as a left-handed pitcher. When he hurt his arm so severely that he could no longer throw with it, he taught himself how to throw with his right arm. He wound up hitting better than .300 in six seasons as a first baseman despite having to wear a brace on his left shoulder.

JUNE 6

1929: San Antonio's Leo Casey clubs two home runs in the Bears' ten-run first inning against the Waco Cubs, leading San Antonio to a 23–3 rout. Casey started the landslide with a three-run homer and closed the inning with a solo shot.

1962: San Antonio's Don Davis ends an eleven-inning strikeout duel with a solo homer, giving the Missions a 1–0 victory over Tulsa. Tulsa's Bill Wakefield struck out seventeen, and San Antonio's Harvey Branch had eleven.

1963: After umpire Tony Ahumada is hit on the head with a wild relay throw, players from Albuquerque and Amarillo help umpire Hank DiJohnson work the game until an amateur umpire arrives.

1967: Austin's Cito Gaston sets a league record by drawing six walks in an eleven-inning game. Gaston made his big-league debut later in 1967 and appeared in 1,026 games in the Majors. He went on to lead the Toronto Blue Jays to two World Series titles as a manager.

1975: Midland's Julio Cesar Gonzalez, a career .262 hitter in the minors, goes six for six with four RBIs in the Cubs' 16–7 rout of El Paso.

1980: Midland's Jesus Alfaro drives in four runs in the first inning of a 13–10 victory over Amarillo. Alfaro had a two-run triple in his first appearance in the ten-run inning and later belted a two-run homer.

1981: Relief pitcher Rafael Pimentel earns victories in both ends of Arkansas' sweep of a double-header against Shreveport. Pimentel won eight games for the Travs in 1981 and had ten saves, a career high.

1987: Arkansas' Matt Kinzer allows just one ball to leave the infield in a 10–0 no-hitter against Tulsa. Kinzer retired the first seventeen batters he faced, and the fly out to center came from Jim St. Laurent to start the seventh. Kinzer pitched in nine games in the Majors in 1989–90, and he also appeared in one game in the NFL, punting for the Detroit Lions in a contest in 1987.

JUNE 7

1902: Corsicana begins a record twenty-seven-game winning streak with a 6–2 victory over Fort Worth. The run included the team's famous 51–3 pounding of Texarkana. Just three pitchers—Belmont Method, Bob White and William "Lucky" Wright—appeared on the mound for Corsicana during the streak.

1930: Wichita Falls' Larry Bettencourt drives in eleven runs in a double-header sweep of Waco. He had a two-run homer and a grand slam in the first game, which finished at 18–1, and he went three for three with two homers in the 11–2 second-game rout.

1947: Houston misses turning a triple play when umpire Fred Sigler rules a trapped sacrifice bunt a foul ball. On the next pitch, Fort Worth's Elmer "Red" Durrett lines into a legitimate triple-killing.

1963: Jerry Hummitzsch fires a no-hitter in the opening game of a double-header as Austin tops Tulsa 2–0. He walked four and struck out seven. Hummitzsch won ten games for Austin in 1963 and struck out 126 in 144 innings.

1994: Midland's Mark Sweeney makes the best of a two-for-two night with six RBIs. Sweeney had a double and a home run, plus a bases-loaded walk and a sacrifice fly. After just fourteen games in the loop, he was promoted to Triple-A.

JUNE 8

1922: Dallas pitcher Roy Mitchell is hit four times by pitches from Houston's A.L. Gheen. Gheen set the league record by hitting two others.

1940: In front of about eight thousand fans—a turnout hurt by bad weather—Dizzy Dean makes his debut for the Tulsa Oilers. Dean limited Fort Worth to six hits. Dean wound up appearing in twenty-one games and going 8-8 and then pitched in ten games for the Chicago Cubs at the end of the schedule.

1955: Tulsa reliever Al Widmar gets the victory in both halves of a double header with Beaumont, giving him three in two nights. Widmar was 18-8 in 1955, appearing in fifty-three games.

1959: Victoria's Frank Howard hits three consecutive three-run homers in a 19–4 rout of Austin. Howard's blasts came in the fifth, sixth and seventh innings. "Hondo" Howard went on to hit 382 home runs in sixteen seasons in the Majors, twice leading the league with forty-four.

Victoria's Frank Howard blasted homers in three consecutive at-bats against Austin in 1959. *Texas League collection.*

1962: Amarillo connects for seven home runs in an 11–5 victory at El Paso, including three by Charlie Keller in four at-bats. The son of legendary slugger "King Kong" Keller went on to hit six more homers in thirty-five games for the Gold Sox in 1962, the twenty-two-year-old's last season in pro ball.

1965: A ruling from league president Hugh Finnerty allows Disch Field organist Ralph Kles to continue playing at Austin's games as long as the tunes are "in good taste." El Paso manager Chuck Tanner had complained about the music during a 13–0 loss.

1967: Albuquerque scores four runs in the first inning before being charged with an official at-bat on the way to a 14–7 rout of Amarillo. The game began with three walks, a sacrifice fly, two more walks, a hit batsman and a catcher's-interference call.

1968: After walking his first two times at the plate, Albuquerque's Willie Crawford hits a triple, a single and two homers, the second of which clears the 425-foot sign in center field by 40 feet, in a 14–7 victory over Amarillo.

1972: Amarillo's Frank Riccelli strikes out 16 in 8.2 innings of a 9–7 victory over Memphis. The left-hander wound up striking out 183 in 164 innings for the Gold Sox in 1972, his best season in baseball.

1976: Midland's Bernie Beckman allows just one man to reach base in throwing a no-hitter in the second game of a double-header at San Antonio. The twenty-five-year-old native of the Netherlands retired thirteen consecutive batters before Rudy Jaramillo reached on an error by first baseman Wayne Tyrone.

1988: San Antonio scores seven runs in the top of the tenth inning to beat Wichita 11–4. All fourteen of the Missions' hits were singles.

June 9

1890: Texas League president Joseph Seinsheimer announces that the league is folding because of financial problems. It would return in 1892.

1931: A bases-loaded single by Houston's Homer Peel turns into a triple play by the Dallas Steers. The runner at third scored, but the man from second stopped halfway between third and home, setting off a string of events that saw seven Dallas fielders take part in a triple play scored 9-2-5-4-3-4-6-4.

1935: Galveston's Eddie Cole pitches the league's first perfect game in a 1–0 win over Tulsa. Bill McGhee's two-out homer in the bottom of the ninth provided the game's only run. Cole played in the minor leagues until 1951, winning 166 games.

1947: Beaumont's John Mackinson walks 11 men but still beats Tulsa 6–1, thanks to eight strikeouts and just three hits. Mackinson ended both the eighth and ninth innings with bases-loaded strikeouts. He led the league with 130 walks in 1947 but still won ten games.

1961: Victoria fans see their new team, the recently relocated Rio Grande Valley Giants, split a double-header against their former team, now representing Ardmore, Oklahoma.

1963: Amarillo's Ron Campbell wrecks Albuquerque, driving in nine runs and going four for six in a 17–10 come-from-behind victory. The Gold Sox won the game with an eight-run rally in the ninth, topped by a two-run double by manager Joe Macko.

1968: El Paso's Bobby Taylor's hitting streak is stopped at thirty-three, three games short of Ike Boone's league record from 1923 (a record passed by Bobby Trevino in 1969). Taylor, Boone, Trevino and Kedzi Kirkham (thirty-three

Player-manager Joe Macko topped off an eight-run, game-winning rally for Amarillo in 1963. *Texas League collection.*

consecutives games in 1922) are the only players in league history with streaks of more than thirty games.

1982: Andy Van Slyke comes up with a three-run homer, two triples and a single in Arkansas' 10–2 victory over Tulsa. Van Slyke went on to play parts of thirteen seasons in the Major Leagues, earn a spot in the All-Star Game three times and win four Gold Gloves.

1985: Midland leadoff man Mark McLemore and number-two hitter Mike Madril both go five for six, accounting for ten of the Angels' twenty-two hits in a 13–12 victory over Beaumont. Madril's single in the bottom of the fourteenth brought in the winning run.

JUNE 10

1908: Fort Worth splits a double-header with Waco despite getting just one hit all day. The Panthers won the first game 3–1, collecting a single off Frank Browning, and were no-hit by spitballer Everett "Pep" Hornsby, older brother of Rogers Hornsby, in the second.

1912: Fort Worth suffers through a second no-hitter in twelve days, falling to Houston's Roscoe Watson 5–0. The Panthers had been blanked by Beaumont on May 31. Pol Perritt was the loser in both games.

1949: Fort Worth's Carl Erskine walks fourteen men but still shuts out Shreveport, 19–0. Erskine wound up pitching twelve seasons for the Dodgers and was a twenty-game winner in 1953.

1969: Memphis's Jim Bibby strikes out 11 Dallas–Fort Worth batters in a 7-inning nightcap of a double-header, winning 2–0. Bibby wound up striking out 180 in 1969, 65 in 75 innings at Class A Tidewater and 115 in 122 innings for Memphis.

2006: Every batter in the Midland lineup has at least one hit, one RBI and one run in an 18–2 blasting of Frisco.

2010: San Antonio's Matt Clark drives in eight of his team's runs in a 10–9 victory over Frisco. Clark had a grand slam in the first inning and a two-run homer in the second.

JUNE 11

1937: Umpire Joe Pate overrules the official scorer on a close play at first base, giving Firpo Marberry of Dallas a 3–0 no-hitter against Galveston.

1965: The Dallas–Fort Worth Spurs begin a string of nine consecutive one-run decisions in seven days, including two double-headers, a thirteen-inning game and a twenty-five-inning game.

1966: Arkansas plays its third seventeen-inning game in a span of eleven days, beating El Paso 5–4. The Travelers had lost to Dallas–Fort Worth in seventeen on June 2 and beat Amarillo in seventeen on June 8.

1969: Arkansas' Reggie Cleveland improves his record to 9-1 with a 3–2 decision over El Paso. His five-hit complete game was his eighth of the season and his seventh in a row.

2006: A crowd of 9,022 turns out to see big-leaguer Roger Clemens on a rehab assignment in Corpus Christi. The forty-three-year-old pitcher held San Antonio scoreless in six innings of work and struck out eleven as the Hooks won 5–1.

JUNE 12

1906: Mike O'Connor, who played thirteen seasons in the league from 1888 to 1905 and managed the Corsicana team that was 88-23 and had a twenty-seven-game winning streak, dies in a state hospital in Austin at the age of forty.

1930: Fort Worth's Lil Stoner strikes out eighteen in a 2–0 no-hitter against San Antonio. Stoner, who won fourteen games for Fort Worth in 1930, allowed just one base runner, a walk in the seventh inning.

1971: A game between Amarillo and Albuquerque is interrupted when tear gas used to help quell a nearby riot drifts into Sports Stadium

Jeff Fassero was 4-1 with a 1.64 ERA and threw a no-hitter while with Arkansas in 1989. *Texas League collection.*

in Albuquerque. At one point, the players left the field, but they returned later to finish the game.

1989: Arkansas pitcher Jeff Fassero throws a no-hitter against Jackson, winning 5–0. Fassero struck out nine, walked one and even hit a home run. He went 4-1 for the Travs with a 1.64 ERA in 1989, earning a promotion to Triple-A, and started a sixteen-year career in the Major Leagues in 1991.

2007: Frisco rallies from a 9–0 deficit to top Midland 13–11. Salomon Manriquez led the RoughRiders' comeback, driving in six runs and hitting two homers, including a three-run walk-off shot in the ninth.

JUNE 13

1961: Austin starter Larry Maxie hurls the first of two nine-inning no-hitters he would toss within thirty-one days as he bests Victoria 2–0. Maxie threw another no-hitter against Poza Rica on July 15, but his career in the Majors lasted exactly two games in 1969.

1968: Five days after the end of his classes at Southern Illinois University, Jerry Reuss throws a two-hit, 2–0 win for Arkansas over Amarillo. Reuss allowed just one runner to advance as far as second base.

Cohen Stadium replaced Dudley Field as the Texas League's home in El Paso in 1990. *Texas League collection.*

1970: Longtime amateur umpire Ed Oliver joins the league's staff on an interim basis. Oliver is deaf and mute, leading league president Bobby Bragan to observe, "If anyone wants to protest a call, he'll have to bring along a pencil and paper."

1990: El Paso opens $6.8 million Cohen Stadium, which replaces sixty-six-year-old Dudley Field. The opening had been delayed from April. The park is named in honor of longtime El Paso baseball promoters Syd and Andy Cohen.

1994: Fernando Valenzuela pitches an inning for the Mexican League All-Stars in their 5–1 loss to the Texas League All-Stars in San Antonio. It is Valenzuela's first playing appearance in San Antonio since he was a nineteen-year-old sensation for the San Antonio Dodgers in 1980.

JUNE 14

1915: A flood puts the Fort Worth ballpark under ten feet of water, forcing the Panthers to transfer a series of games to Galveston. Since the club also lost all its gear, it had to borrow uniforms from Dallas.

1921: Galveston's Pete Lapan goes six for six, including two home runs, in a 15–9 victory over Wichita Falls. The game marked a distinct change in the thirty-year-old catcher's career; he had never hit higher than

Pete Lapan went six for six for Galveston on June 14, 1921. *Texas League collection.*

.238 before 1921, but he went on to hit .263 for Galveston in 1921, .335 for Little Rock of the Southern Association in 1922 and a career-best .367 for Wichita Falls in 1929.

1922: Five straight Galveston batters hit home runs in the fifth inning of a 12–11 squeaker over Wichita Falls.

1955: Oklahoma City's Frank Barnes becomes the first African American Texas League pitcher to throw a no-hitter as he beats Shreveport 1–0. Barnes appeared in the Texas League, the International League and the American Association in 1955.

JUNE 15

Jay Clarke hit eight home runs in eight at-bats in Corsicana's record-shattering 51–3 victory over Texarkana. *Texas League collection.*

1902: Corsicana catcher Jay Clarke hits eight home runs in eight at-bats against Texarkana, leading his club to a record 51–3 victory in a game played in Ennis, Texas, because Sunday ball was banned at Corsicana. Corsicana had fifty-three hits, twenty-one home runs, forty-five RBIs and twenty-five extra-base hits, all single-game league records.

1948: San Antonio third baseman Charlie Grant drives in nine runs with a single, a triple and a grand slam as the Missions rout Dallas 26–7. Grant hit .297 for the Missions in 1948, midway through a fifteen-season pro career.

1954: Fort Worth's Calvin Felix drives in five runs after entering the game as a pinch hitter in a 12–7 victory over Beaumont. Felix hit a grand slam in his first time to the plate in the Cats' ten-run ninth inning and then singled in a run when he came up again.

1967: Dallas–Fort Worth manager Jo-Jo White, still upset about a call the previous day, is ejected during the exchange of lineups before the game.

1996: Midland rallies from a fourteen-run deficit to beat El Paso 17–16. After trailing 16–2, the Angels scored two in the fourth, one in the fifth, one in the sixth, two in the seventh, two in the eighth and seven in the bottom of the ninth to get the victory. (The largest comeback in Major League history is twelve.) The Angels overcame a six-run deficit the next night to beat the Diablos 14–13.

1998: Tyrone Horne hits a home run to lead off the bottom of the tenth inning, giving Arkansas its first lead of the game and a 21–20 victory over Jackson.

2006: Each member of the Wichita lineup has at least one hit, one RBI and one run scored in a 15–1 romp over Arkansas.

2009: Corpus Christi batters strike out nineteen times against four San Antonio pitchers and still come away with a 6–0 victory over the Missions. San Antonio starter Mat Latos whiffed twelve in 5.1 innings.

POWER SHOWS

Just six players have hit four or more home runs in a single Texas League game, led by Jay Clarke's eight on June 15, 1902, in Corsicana's 51–3 victory over Texarkana. Clyde "Sis" Bateman, Ardmore's Al Nagel, El Paso's Charlie Dees, El Paso's Tom Brunansky and Arkansas' Tyrone Horne each hit four.

JUNE 16

1929: San Antonio abuses three Wichita Falls pitchers in the first inning, scoring twelve runs on the way to a 23–3 victory. Dutch Wetzel got two of the Indians' eight hits in the inning, both of which drove in a pair of runs.

1946: Houston's Jim Basso hits into three consecutive double plays in a game with the Dallas Rebels. Basso appeared in the minors for thirteen seasons, missing the 1942–45 seasons because of World War II. The outfielder played in cities including Sioux City, South Dakota; Paris, Texas; and Nuevo Laredo, Mexico.

1965: Austin beats Dallas–Fort Worth 2–1 in twenty-five innings in the longest game ever played at Arlington's Turnpike Stadium. The game was the longest in league history until 1988.

1965: Albuquerque's Don Sutton gives up just three hits and strikes out thirteen in beating El Paso 3–2. The twenty-year-old right-hander retired the last sixteen men he faced. Sutton went a combined 23-7 with a 2.35 ERA in 1965, including an 8-1 record with a 1.51 ERA at Class-A Santa Barbara. Sutton made his big-league debut in 1966, launching a career that saw him win 324 games and then earn election to the National Baseball Hall of Fame in 1998.

2013: Northwest Arkansas position players got the win and the save in the Nationals' 3–2 victory over Arkansas. Mitch Canham pitched the eleventh and twelfth innings for his first career victory, and Whit Merrifield earned a save in his first professional pitching appearance in the thirteenth.

JUNE 17

1923: Houston leadoff hitter Ed "Dutch" Sperber hits for the cycle and drives in seven runs in the Buffs' 14–0 whitewash of Wichita Falls. Sperber went four for five and was in the middle of all three Houston rallies in the game. He drove in a run in the second with a single, two more in the sixth with a triple and four more in the seventh with a grand slam.

1932: San Antonio's League Park burns to the ground following an afternoon game. At one point, a crowd of about twenty thousand watched the blaze, which also consumed several nearby buildings. The club played at Brackenridge High School's Eagle Field on June 19 and then completed the season at Tech Field, which became the team's home through 1946.

1946: A close call at first base that gave Houston the go-ahead run in the top of the ninth inning provokes Fort Worth fans to shower LaGrave Field with bottles for twenty-five minutes. After the field was finally cleared up, Houston retired Fort Worth one-two-three in the bottom of the ninth and took home a 5–4 victory.

1996: San Antonio's Paul Konerko launches a seven-day home-run streak with a blast against Wichita. He hit two more on June 18 and three on June 20 and wound up with ten hits, six homers, a double, a triple, ten RBIs and eight runs for the week. The first baseman made his big-league debut in 1997, and since then he has won a World Series ring with the Chicago White Sox and has appeared in the All-Star Game six times.

1989: Chris Cron and John Orton drive in six runs each to lead Midland past El Paso 22–4. Cron had a single, two doubles and a home run. Orton brought home his runs on a pair of homers. Cron led the league in RBIs (103) and doubles (thirty-three).

San Antonio's Paul Konerko had ten hits—including six homers, a double and a triple—ten RBIs and eight runs in the span of a week in 1996. *Photo by Tom Kayser.*

JUNE 18

1904: Fort Worth edges Corsicana 1–0 in a game finished with Fort Worth pitcher Charlie Jackson acting as the umpire. Regular umpire Bill Cowell had declared a forfeit in favor of Fort Worth in the second after a dispute about a hit, but after Cowell left the field, the teams agreed to play the game to completion with Jackson calling balls and strikes.

1930: Dallas signs big-league veteran Grover Cleveland Alexander to a then-record salary of $1,660 a month. Alexander would go 1-2 in just five games for the Steers before retiring.

1947: Beaumont's Charlie Glunt is thrown out at the plate three times in the same game. Glunt was attempting to score from second base on singles in the first, eighth and twelfth innings.

Pitcher Grover Cleveland Alexander had a short and mostly unsuccessful stint in the league in 1930. *Photo Courtesy Bain News Service Archives, Library of Congress.*

1950: Oklahoma City's Jim Lemon wraps up a nine-day streak that saw him hit seven home runs, including three in one game. Lemon finished the season with thirty-nine homers and went on to a twelve-year big-league career that included being named to the 1960 All-Star Game.

1958: Running short on players, Victoria signs the team's thirty-year-old groundskeeper, John Faucett, to a contract. The catcher walked in his first time at the plate and appeared in twenty-four games.

1962: El Paso's Carl Boles hits three home runs and drives in six runs in a 14–10 victory over Albuquerque. Boles made his big-league debut for the San Francisco Giants in August but appeared in just nineteen games. He returned to the minors in 1963 and then played six seasons (1966–71) in Japan.

1967: Former big-leaguer Duke Snider receives the first suspension of his twenty-three-year career following a run-in with umpire Frank Walsh. Snider's Albuquerque Dodgers went from fourth place in June to first at the end of the season.

1969: Memphis right-hander Bob Johnson throws his third straight complete game and third straight shutout, blanking Arkansas 3–0. Johnson had been sent down from Triple-A because he couldn't finish a game. He went 13-4 with thirteen complete games in seventeen starts for the Blues and had an ERA of 1.48.

1980: El Paso's Tom Brunansky hits four consecutive home runs and drives in nine runs to lead the Diablos' 19–9 romp over Midland. The nineteen-year-old center fielder had not hit a home run in the previous twenty-three games.

1997: Scott Krause of El Paso goes five for five with three home runs and drives in seven runs as the Diablos pound Midland 14–6. Krause hit .361 for the Diablos in 1997 but remarkably did not claim the batting title. Teammate Mike Kinkade came in at .385, which was the highest in the league since Waco's Del Pratt hit .386 in 1927.

2000: The Texas League All-Stars pound their Mexican League counterparts 12–2 in front of 7,236 fans at El Paso. The Diablos' Alex Cabrera, with two doubles and three RBIs, was the game's MVP.

2003: Pitchers from Frisco and Tulsa combine to tie a league record, hitting six batters. The Drillers' C.J. Wilson hit three, and teammate Keith Stamler hit three more.

2009: Tulsa sets a league record by recording three consecutive sacrifice flies—on four pitches—in an 11–2 victory over Northwest Arkansas. On the second sac fly, Ryan Harvey got credit for bringing in Jeff Kindel even though center fielder Jose Duarte dropped the ball.

JUNE 19

1961: Amarillo shuts out San Antonio for twenty-five straight innings of a double-header and sweeps the Missions, 2–0 and 2–1. The Missions post one hit in the seven-inning first game and do not score their sole run until the bottom of the nineteenth in the nightcap.

1961: Austin's Larry Maxie loses for the first time in 1961, falling 2–1 in eleven innings to Victoria. Maxie won seventeen games for Austin in 1961 and had a league-best 2.08 ERA.

1997: The first three hitters in Tulsa's lineup—Cesar Morillo, Edwin Diaz and Fernando Tatis—each get four hits and each score three runs in a 19–8 rout of Shreveport. Tatis also drove in six runs with three homers.

JUNE 20

1908: Fred (Winchell) Cook, San Antonio's right-handed submariner, does not allow a ball out of the infield for ten innings but then loses a no-hitter in the eleventh and falls to Waco 2–0 in the thirteenth. The runs scored after Cook had thrown a double-play ball into center field.

1929: Fort Worth right fielder Larman Cox doubles four times and goes five for five in the Cats' 15–5 victory over San Antonio. Cox recorded forty-seven doubles for the season, second to the fifty-one recorded by Dallas's Randy Moore.

1930: Waco blanks Fort Worth 13–0 in the first regular-season night game in league history. Many Texas League dignitaries joined the 3,500 paid customers at Katy Field to examine the franchise's $7,500 investment in lighting. By the end of the season, night games also had been played at Houston, San Antonio and Shreveport.

1942: Fort Worth's Alex Hooks goes ten innings without taking a throw at first base. In the Cats' 3–2 victory over San Antonio, Hooks handled three pop-ups and had an assist on a toss to pitcher Claude Horton.

1965: Dallas–Fort Worth center fielder Don Young turns in a remarkable play, chasing down a long drive by Amarillo's Leon McFadden. While racing back, Young slipped, dropped to his knee and lost his glove but then recovered to make a barehanded catch near the fence.

1997: Tulsa's Dan Collier's streak of hitting home runs in seven consecutive games is snapped. It was only the third time the feat was accomplished in minor-league history. Collier hit a career-best twenty-six homers in 1997.

JUNE 21

1910: Galveston pitcher Bert Hise loses to Shreveport 1–0 when he uncorks a wild pitch in the tenth inning. The wild pitch came with two outs and two strikes on Rube Gardner.

1924: For the second time in just over two years, Wichita Falls loses its ballpark to a fire. The blaze, believed to have begun in a cushion storeroom, destroyed the two-year-old structure.

1930: Shreveport establishes a league record with seven sacrifices in a game against Beaumont.

1930: Gene Moore drives in eight runs with two homers and two singles to lead Dallas's 21–4 romp over Waco. "Rowdy" Moore would hit .352 for the season, and he wound up playing fourteen seasons in the Majors, appearing in the 1937 All-Star Game and the 1944 World Series.

1935: Tulsa's Al Shealy throws the first perfect game in league history, leading the Oilers to a 7–0 victory over San Antonio in the seven-inning second game of a double-header. Eddie Cole of Shreveport would throw the league's first nine-inning perfect game just seventeen days later, on July 10.

1961: Victoria's Danilo Rivas strikes out 18 San Antonio batters but still loses 4–3 in 10 innings. Rivas struck out 127 in 138 innings in 1961.

1969: El Paso's Bobby Trevino triples twice, doubles twice and singles, driving in seven runs in the Sun Kings' 13–2 victory over Arkansas. It would be his last season in the United States; he returned to his native Mexico in 1970 and played ten more seasons in the Mexican League.

2004: For the third time in league history, the All-Star Game ends in a tie. El Paso's Marland Williams scored the tying run for the West in the eighth inning, but his real highlight was an inside-the-park homer in the third.

THAT FAMILIAR FEELING

Tim Ireland, who managed both Frisco and El Paso, was involved in two ties in the Texas League All-Star Game. *Texas League collection.*

The Texas League All-Star Game has ended in a tie three times—1993, 2002 and 2004—and there are two striking similarities about the first two: a 3–3 score and veteran Texas League manager Tim Ireland, who was at both. Ireland was the West Division manager in 1993, when he was at El Paso, and in 2002, when he led Tulsa.

JUNE 22

1951: Tulsa knocks off Houston 2–1 despite getting just one hit. That single by Johnny Temple led off the second inning. Temple stole second and went to third on a passed ball. Alex Grammas walked, and then Temple and Grammas pulled off a double steal for the first run. On the next pitch, Grammas stole third and then came home when the throw to third flew into left field.

1979: Two days after suffering with a 104-degree fever, Tulsa's Len Whitehouse completes a double-header sweep, throwing a no-hitter to beat Shreveport 2–0.

1990: San Antonio leadoff hitter Tom Goodwin goes five for five, scores three times, drives in two runs and steals four bases in the Missions' 11–8 victory over Wichita. Goodwin led the league with 60 steals in 1990 and went on to steal 369 bases in fourteen seasons in the Majors.

1998: Wichita's Carlos Mendez doubles in his seventh consecutive game and records his twelfth double in the last thirteen games. Mendez hit .319 in fifty-two games for the Wranglers before he was promoted to Triple-A.

2006: Midland's Kurt Suzuki drives in eight runs in a wild 15–10 victory at Tulsa. The catcher piled up the RBIs with a run-scoring single, a three-run triple and a grand slam.

JUNE 23

1903: Fort Worth's Billy Disch steals home against Paris in the eighth inning to tie the game at one and then scores the game-winning run in the tenth on a single by George Reitz. Disch played seven minor-league seasons between 1902 and 1911 but earned his fame as baseball coach at the University of Texas (1911–39), where he went 513-180-12 and won twenty Southwest Conference titles.

1917: Dallas's Snipe Conley wins his seventeenth consecutive game with a no-hitter in the first game of a double-header with Fort Worth. Conley receives $250, collected for him by the Dallas Rooters' Club.

1943: Tulsa's Paul Easterling hits three home runs in three consecutive at-bats off three different pitchers in an 11–2 romp at Houston.

1960: Four Victoria players have four hits each in a 22–6 pounding of Veracruz. The Rosebuds wound up with twenty-eight hits.

1961: Amarillo turns a wild triple play in a 4–3 victory over Austin. With John Garafalo at first and Bill Lucas at second, attempting a double steal, Tippy

Johnson struck out. Catcher Rich Winsle's throw to third arrived well ahead of Lucas, and Lucas retreated to second—where Garafalo was standing. As Amarillo second baseman Don Bummer began to chase Garafalo back to first, Lucas took off for third. Bummer stopped and threw to shortstop Phil Linz, who tagged out Lucas and then fired the ball to first baseman Chuck Burheller, who tagged out Garafalo.

1991: In a West Texas shootout, Midland scores five runs in the eighth inning to top El Paso 20–18. Midland had twenty-three hits and El Paso twenty-two in a game that took four hours and seventeen minutes to play. The contest became the longest nine-inning game in league history.

JUNE 24

Tulsa's Tony York reached base in fourteen consecutive plate appearances in 1937. *Texas League collection.*

1889: Jess Derrick of Waco throws the first no-hitter in league history, beating Austin 3–0. Derrick finished the season with a more-dubious distinction, going 13-24 to become the league's first twenty-game loser.

1928: Shreveport's Ziggy Sears was almost perfect in a double-header sweep of Waco, recording a hit in his first seven plate appearances in the games and finishing seven for eight.

1937: Tulsa's Tony York begins a streak that would see him reach base in fourteen consecutive plate appearances, setting a league record. York finished with seven singles, five doubles and two walks over a span of four games. The Texan went on to play in the minors until the age of forty-three in 1956.

1946: San Antonio pulls off a 4-2-5-4 triple play in a 2–1 loss to Tulsa. With the bases loaded in the fifth, Tulsa's Joe Rullo hit a grounder to second baseman Stan Galle. Galle threw home for the force play. Catcher Mike Sertich threw to third baseman Pete Kraus for the second out, and then Kraus threw to Galle to get a force play at second.

1951: Tommy Fine of San Antonio walks the first Tulsa batter he faces and then retires the next twenty-one in a row for a 2–0 no-hitter against Tulsa in the first game of a double-header. Fine won seventeen games for the Missions in 1951.

1958: Corpus Christi catcher/manager Ray Murray hits a two-run homer off Tulsa manager Al Widman, who is pitching in relief, as the Giants win 8–6.

1986: Shreveport's Mackey Sasser hits for the cycle, with the double scoring the winning run in the thirteenth inning of a 2–1 victory at Jackson.

1988: El Paso PA man Paul Strelzin is ejected when, after a close play, he plays part of a Linda Ronstadt song that includes the phrase "I've been cheated."

JUNE 25

1906: Two of the scheduled three games in the league are no-hitters, as Ed Rodebaugh of Dallas no-hits Cleburne 3–1, and Fort Worth's Alex Dupree throws his second hitless game of the season in whitewashing Waco 1–0.

1922: Nic "Coo-Coo" DeMaggio goes six for six as Beaumont tops Wichita Falls 15–7. DeMaggio, Beaumont's left fielder, stroked four singles and two triples. DeMaggio hit a combined .352 for Dallas and Beaumont in 1922, a career high.

1946: Shreveport tops Dallas 9–2 in a game that required intervention by the Dallas police. Rebels manager Al Vincent had to be escorted from the field by police after a long argument. Once Vincent was gone, fans showered the field with beer bottles, and police had to restrain fans from attacking the umpires.

1964: Albuquerque's Mel Corbo posts his second five-RBI game of the week, going four for five in a 14–3 romp over El Paso. On June 21, Corbo hit a grand slam and a run-scoring double in a 14–5 victory over Austin. Corbo went on to win the league batting title at .339.

1966: Amarillo beats Dallas–Fort Worth 9–5 despite getting just six hits. The Spurs committed three errors, and their pitchers walked seven and uncorked a wild pitch.

JUNE 26

1914: Houston runners steal seven bases in one inning during a 12–0 romp over Austin.

1923: Wichita Falls and Galveston combine for forty-three hits in a game the Sand Crabs won 17–13 in eleven innings. Don Brown and Ed Kearns were both five for six for the winners, and Brown scored six times.

1938: Facing each other for the first time since the 1934 World Series, Beaumont's Schoolboy Rowe and Dallas's Paul Dean put on a pitching duel, with Rowe winning 2–1 in front of 9,400 fans in Beaumont.

1949: One-armed outfielder Pete Gray, thirty-two, is released by Dallas and retires from the game. Gray appeared in forty-four games, hitting .214 for the Eagles, and resumed operation of a billiard hall he owned in Nanticoke, Pennsylvania.

1977: San Antonio rallies from an 8–0 deficit to beat El Paso 9–8 in seventeen innings. The Diablos had two runners thrown out at the plate in the top of the seventeenth, and then the Dodgers won in the bottom of the inning when Terry Farr scored on a bouncer back to the mound.

1998: In his second start with Wichita after earning a roster spot in a tryout, Scott Taylor pitches an impressive seven innings in the Wranglers' 11–1 win over El Paso. Taylor, released twice from Triple-A clubs in 1998, wound up going 7-3 for his hometown team in his final minor-league season.

1998: The San Antonio Missions take a 4–0 lead in the first inning on just eight pitches, as Charlie Nelson, Tony Mota and Peter Bergeron all single in front of Angel Pena's grand slam on the eighth pitch of the inning.

2001: Hank Blalock, in just his sixth Texas League game, hits for the cycle to propel Tulsa to an 8–1 win over Midland. Blalock would hit for the cycle again on June 28. It is thought that no other player has hit for the cycle twice in one minor-league season.

2013: Max Stassi drives in eight runs with two homers—including a grand slam—and a double, leading Corpus Christi over Springfield 13–1.

JUNE 27

1932: Future Hall of Famer George Sisler resigns as manager in Tyler. The club was 26-51 at the time and finished 57-93, forty-two and a half games behind the regular-season champs, Beaumont.

1955: Ryne Duren strikes out eighteen batters in his debut with San Antonio and wins 1–0. Beaumont's Pete Modica was a tough-luck loser, yielding the lone run of the game in the top of the ninth on a walk, a hit batter and a throwing error on the back end of a double play attempt that would have ended the inning.

1971: Four Shreveport pitchers combine to strike out sixteen

George Sisler managed in the league in 1932. *Photo Courtesy Bain News Service Archives, Library of Congress.*

San Antonio Missions executive Dave Oldham presents a cowboy hat and boots to manager Ron Roenicke in 1998. *Photo by Tom Kayser.*

Memphis batters in a 7–5 victory. Starter Bruce Heinbechner whiffed seven in 4.1 innings, Terry Cox got three in 2 innings, Moe Oiger one in one-third inning and Dave Sells five in 2.2 innings.

1997: The St. Louis Cardinals' Tom Pagnozzi, on a rehab assignment at Arkansas, goes four for five with two home runs and six RBIs in a 10–5 victory over Tulsa.

1998: After winning the 1997 pennant and the first half in 1998, San Antonio manager Ron Roenicke is promoted to Triple-A Albuquerque when Albuquerque manager Glenn Hoffman is promoted to replace fired Dodgers manager Bill Russell.

2013: Northwest Arkansas' Brooks Pounders allows just two base runners, tossing a no-hitter and topping Midland 11–0. He hit one man, and another reached on an error.

JUNE 28

1897: Paris is caught in the act of trying to get a game rained out, winding up with a 9–0 forfeit loss to Dallas. The Parasites trailed 10–0 after four innings, but they observed a storm on the horizon that would have rained out the game before it was official. So Paris engaged in what observers called "sloppy and indifferent" play, including allowing an uncontested double steal. Umpire Ed Clark would have none of it, awarding Dallas a 9–0 forfeit victory.

1914: Houston steals fourteen bases in an 11–0 romp over Austin, which was using a local amateur pitcher, Bert Rorer. Every Houston player but one had a steal, and pitcher Roger Edmondson stole twice.

1920: Galveston's Doc Waldbauer walks sixteen men, including two with the bases loaded in the bottom of the ninth inning, in a 5–4 loss to Shreveport.

1931: Houston pitcher Dizzy Dean wins both ends of a double-header at Fort Worth, taking the first game 12–3 and throwing a three-hit, 3–0 whitewash in the second. The games were witnessed by more than six thousand fans, including Dean's wife, who had arrived by plane on the morning of the games.

1962: A crowd of 5,168 at Austin's Disch Field sees a squad made up of Austin and Tulsa players whip the Houston Colt .45s 8–1. Austin manager Jimmy Brown and Tulsa skipper Whitey Kurowski used twenty-nine players in the exhibition, including seven pitchers.

1965: The Los Angeles Angels rout their Double-A affiliate, the El Paso Sun Kings, 16–8 in front of nearly six thousand fans at Dudley Field.

1971: The Texas League board of directors votes to return to an eight-team format in 1972, but it wouldn't be easy. The league would lose Albuquerque and Dallas–Fort Worth at the end of the season but would gain El Paso, Lafayette and Midland.

1985: Jackson beats Tulsa 3–2 in sixteen innings in a game featuring two dubious records: most men left on base by both teams (forty-five) and most walks by one team (seventeen, by Tulsa).

OCCUPATIONAL THERAPY

Throughout Texas League history, teams have had an assortment of unusual nicknames, from the Houston Babies to the Longview Cannibals. But many of the nicknames have ties to local industries or businesses:

The Austin Senators earned their nickname because Austin is the state capital.

The club in Beaumont was named both the Oilers and Roughnecks through the years, thanks to the oilfields in southeast Texas.

Cleburne was nicknamed the Railroaders because the town was a hub of railroad lines at the time (1903).

The league had the Corsicana Oil Citys (1902–04) and Oilers (1905), thanks to the East Texas oil boom.

The location of the state's oldest institution of higher learning, Austin College in Sherman, was the inspiration for the Sherman-Denison Students (1902).

The Texarkana Casket Makers were named for the town's largest industry at the time (1902).

Nearby oilfields also inspired the Tulsa Oilers (1933–42, 1946–65) and Drillers (1977–present).

The Wichita Pilots were so named because the city is a midwestern hub for aircraft construction and maintenance (1987–88).

A North Texas oil boom was the inspiration for the Wichita Falls Spudders (1920–32)—a reference to an oilfield job.

JUNE 29

1896: Fort Worth sends twenty-four men to the plate and scores nineteen runs in the fourth inning of a 31–4 victory over Galveston, two records that still stand.

1897: In the last night contest for nearly thirty-three years, Houston and San Antonio play an exhibition under temporary lights at San Pedro Park. The benefit for the Belknap Rifles, a San Antonio military drill group, attracted just over 1,500 fans. A second game under the lights on June 30 drew only 300.

1906: Walter "Hickory" Dickson tosses a no-hitter for Cleburne against Temple, winning the first game of a double-header 5–1. In the nightcap, future Hall of Famer Tris Speaker, usually the Cleburne right fielder, pitches and beats Temple 10–3.

Tris Speaker, one of the game's great hitters, also pitched on occasion for Cleburne in 1906. *Photo Courtesy Bain News Service Archives, Library of Congress.*

1907: Houston Mudcats first baseman Tom "Tacks" Parrott commits five errors in a game with Fort Worth. Parrott, a former Major Leaguer, gave up the game at the end of the season and, after umpiring in 1908, spent several years playing with a Dallas orchestra.

1907: Temple right fielder Harry "Trapper" Longley goes seven for seven in the Boll Weevils' 23–4 victory over Galveston.

1941: Morris Block, the former owner of the San Antonio club, dies. After buying the San Antonio team of the South Texas League for $700 in 1904, Block had been instrumental in the merger of the league with the Texas League in 1907.

1947: Al Rosen drives in eight runs and Oklahoma City scores six runs in the bottom of the ninth to top Fort Worth 13–12 in the first game of a double-header. Rosen's game was no fluke; he led the league with a .349 average in 1947.

1960: Manny Mota singles in the winning run in the bottom of the nineteenth to give Rio Grande Valley a 3–2 victory over the Mexico City Reds—one day after the Reds beat the Giants in sixteen innings.

1962: El Paso's Jesus Alou ends a streak in which he hit safely in forty-eight of forty-nine games. The nineteen-year-old went 81 for 221, a .367 average, during the run.

1965: El Paso outfielder Charlie Dees goes 0 for 4 against Amarillo to end a ten-game hitting streak. Dees was 24 for 37 during the games, a .649 average.

1968: Making his first start of the season, Paul Doyle pitches a no-hitter as Dallas–Fort Worth beats El Paso 4–0. It was the first no-hitter at Turnpike Stadium and the longest appearance of the season for Doyle.

1970: San Antonio commits five errors in the fourth inning and eight overall in a 12–0 loss to Arkansas.

2004: Tulsa's Ryan Shealy hits three-run homers in back-to-back innings in a 14–3 victory at El Paso. Shealy went five for six and also had two doubles.

JUNE 30

1920: Longtime minor-league pitcher Floyd "Rube" Kroh begins a league-record sixteen-game losing streak, spread over time with Houston, Shreveport and Galveston. Kroh finished the season 3-21 but with an ERA of just 3.16.

1929: Shreveport bats around twice—once in the ten-run first inning and again in the seven-run eighth—in a 21–11 pounding of San Antonio. The Missions also managed to bat around once, sending eleven men to the plate in an eight-run ninth inning.

1936: Houston Buffs star Harold Epps establishes a league record with four consecutive sacrifices in a nine-inning game against Tulsa.

1953: Ryne Duren of San Antonio walks eleven, including one with the bases loaded, but finishes with a seven-inning, 4–1 no-hitter against Beaumont.

1954: The Texas League buys the contracts of umpires Jim Odom from the South Atlantic League and Bill Valentine from the Big State League. Both would go on to work in the American League.

1990: The El Paso Diablos dedicate their new ballpark, Cohen Stadium. The park was named in honor of Syd and Andy Cohen, longtime baseball men, who both had died the previous year.

July

JULY 1

1929: Dallas outfielder Simon "Sy" Rosenthal strikes out, ending a streak of 192 at-bats without a strikeout. Rosenthal was a .333 hitter in thirteen minor-league seasons.

1931: Galveston shortstop Keith Molesworth plays both ends of a double-header, sixteen innings, without a single fielding chance.

1989: El Paso scores four times in the bottom of the tenth to top San Antonio, 13–12, on nickel hot-dog night. A reported seventeen thousand hot dogs were sold during the game, which took three hours and forty-five minutes to play.

1991: El Paso rocks San Antonio reliever Isidro Marquez for five hits and three runs in the bottom of the ninth inning to top the Missions 12–11. San Antonio's Eric Young went five for five with four stolen bases in the game, on his way to a league-high seventy steals for the season.

1996: Midland Angels catcher Ben Molina ties a league record by throwing out five Wichita runners attempting to steal. Molina joined three other catchers in the league record book; the last time five runners were thrown out in a game was in 1931.

Midland catcher Ben Molina threw out five men trying to steal on July 1, 1996. *Texas League collection.*

2003: El Paso's Josh Kroeger drops a fly ball, leading to four unearned runs, in his Texas League debut against Round Rock. But the twenty-year-old showed later why he had been promoted, hitting a game-winning, two-run homer in the bottom of the ninth of an 8–6 victory.

JULY 2

1905: Dallas left-hander Harry Ables shuts out Fort Worth 6–0 and 8–0 in a double-header. It was the league's first "iron man" effort, in which a pitcher started and won both games of a double-header.

1937: Beaumont steals nine bases off San Antonio backup catcher Frank Cox yet still needs twelve innings to win 4–3.

1946: Shreveport's Earl Dothager, released by the Houston Buffs less than a month earlier, throws a no-hitter against his former club in the second game of a double-header.

1958: San Antonio starter Bill Bell is charged with six wild pitches in 2.1 innings of a 13–0 loss to Fort Worth. Reliever Roger Aldredge gave up eleven runs on eleven hits and threw two more wild pitches in 4.2 innings.

1965: Ernie Foli and Walt Williams hit inside-the-park homers as Tulsa outslugs Dallas–Fort Worth 18–9. Foli's traveled no more than two hundred feet in the air but bounced under the right fielder's glove and rolled all the way to the fence.

1966: Dallas–Fort Worth ace Fred Norman strikes out 15 and gives up just two hits in beating El Paso 2–1. Norman whiffed the first eight hitters he faced, and he would finish 1966 as the league strikeout leader with 198.

1967: A backup umpire and two players acting as umps get more than they expect when the game between Dallas–Fort Worth and Austin goes fifteen innings. The regular umpire for the game, Bob Henrion, fell ill in the seventh inning. So his partner, Joe Murphy, a substitute for an umpire who was on military duty, moved behind the plate. Austin's Joe Cisterna was called on to umpire at third, and the Spurs' Archie Reynolds became the umpire at first. They worked until the Braves' Bob Turzilli hit a three-run homer in the fifteenth to give Austin a 4–1 victory.

2001: Carlos Hernandez and Wilfredo Rodriguez combine to strike out eighteen Arkansas batters as Round Rock pounds the Travelers 12–2.

JULY 3

1889: Austin hosts Houston in the league's first double-header. The Senators won both games, 13–9 and 5–2.

1902: Argus J. "Lefty" Hamilton of Dallas throws the league's second no-hitter, defeating Fort Worth 3–0 in the first game of a double-header. Hamilton went 12-8 for the Griffins in his only season as a pitcher.

1923: Galveston pitchers begin a streak of four consecutive shutouts in the second game of a double-header with Houston, winning 1–0 behind Lefty Graham. The next day, Hal Deviney blanked the Buffs 2–0. On July 8, Parson Perryman won 1-0, and Graham came back the next day to win 8–0 in the first game of a double-header. The streak ended in the third inning of the second game.

1980: Three runs wind up scoring on a bases-loaded sacrifice fly by Tulsa's Ron Gooch. Mike Jerschele came in from third, colliding with catcher Stan Hough. Right fielder Archie Amerson's throw was off line, allowing George Wright, who had been on second, to score. Pitcher Tom Thurberg, backing up the play, threw wildly, hitting on-deck batter Phil Klimas and allowing Mel Barrow, who had started on first base, to trot home.

1993: Tulsa designated hitter Trey McCoy has two doubles, two homers and eight RBIs in five at-bats as the Drillers beat Jackson 18–6. Tulsa scored twelve times in the second inning, including a two-run single and a two-run homer by McCoy.

2001: After losing in San Antonio in seventeen innings on July 2, Shreveport travels home and winds up playing eighteen innings against Tulsa. Shreveport catcher Guillermo Rodriguez pitched the fifteenth, sixteenth and seventeenth innings, allowing just two runners. Jeremy Luster, who started the game at first, took the loss, giving up two walks and two hits in the eighteenth.

JULY 4

1902: Corsicana shuts out Waco 3–0 for its twenty-seventh win in a row, a professional baseball record at the time.

1931: Shreveport's Ralph Winegarner drives in seven runs in a double-header sweep at Dallas despite getting just two hits. He brought home two runs with groundouts in the first game and then had a two-run single and a three-run homer in the second. The right-hander made it to the Majors but not on the strength of his bat; he pitched in sixty-one games for the Cleveland Indians from 1932 to 1936 and then nine more for the St. Louis Browns in 1949.

1963: Austin's Pat House throws a two-hitter and hits the first home run of his career in a 1–0 victory over El Paso. House retired the last seventeen hitters in order.

1979: After leadoff man Steve Smith reaches base on an error, San Antonio's Rick Goulding retires the next twenty-seven hitters in a row for a no-hitter against Amarillo. The game was the highlight of a six-year minor-league career for the right-hander.

1982: Tulsa turns a ricochet into a triple play in a 7–3 victory over Jackson. With the bases loaded, Al Pedrique lined a drive off the glove of pitcher Kevin Richards. Second baseman Steve Buechele snared the ball on the fly and flipped to shortstop Curtis Wilkerson at second. Wilkerson fired to Mike Jerschele at third for the final out.

1996: El Paso's Sean Maloney begins a string of fourteen saves in fourteen appearances. He would finish the season with thirty-eight saves, at the time a league record.

2007: Frisco claims both a home and a road victory in one day, completing a suspended game in a half inning with a leadoff home run to beat Arkansas 1–0 and then taking the regularly scheduled contest at Dickey-Stephens Park 3–0 on a one-hitter by Armando Galarraga.

Umpire Frank Coe narrowly escaped injury in a car accident in 1937. *Texas League collection.*

JULY 5

1910: Harry Ables of San Antonio and Arthur Loudell of Waco pitch all twenty-three innings of a 1–1 tie at San Antonio. Ables gave up his run in the first inning and went on to strike out seventeen and allow sixteen hits. Loudell struck out eleven and gave up fifteen hits.

1910: Waco hires Texas Christian University coach Ellis Hardy as manager for the 1911 season. Hardy wound up managing the Navigators for eight seasons, going 640-487 and winning outright pennants in 1914 and 1915 and a shared title in 1913.

1937: League umpires Frank Coe, Uley Walsh and Tony Defate escape injury in a car accident near Denton and report for duty. Meanwhile, umpire Chet Fowler missed his assignment in San Antonio, the result of another auto mishap.

1942: Henry "Prince" Oana throws a no-hitter as Fort Worth tops Dallas 6–0. Oana, who starred both as an outfielder and a pitcher, was 42-17 in five Texas League seasons as a pitcher and hit .260.

1942: Oklahoma City pitcher/utility man Red Traback decides he has had enough, storming off the mound with two outs in the seventh inning, showering, dressing and going home. Traback, who had started the game in right field, came into the game in relief in the fifth inning. When he departed, he had given up nine runs, most of them unearned, in what turned out to be a 16–2 loss to Tulsa.

1963: San Antonio sends fourteen men to the plate in a nine-run first inning and cruises to a 13–6 romp over El Paso. Jim Pendleton had a three-run homer in the first for the Bullets, and Jerry Grote drove in four runs with a single, a double and a homer.

1968: In the midst of a 13–3 loss in Albuquerque, the San Antonio Missions pull a sit-in strike. Umpire Larry Barnett ordered the bench cleared after a nineteen-minute argument, but the players refused to leave. Finally, the city's fire code was imposed and the players were threatened with arrest for blocking a fire exit.

1972: Arkansas pitcher Rudy Arroyo is pulled off an American Airlines flight after making a crack about a bomb. Arroyo, who had to take a later flight, pitched that night and lost 5–0. He then had to write a letter of apology to the FBI, American Airlines and the Little Rock Police Department and explain the incident to his father, an American Airlines employee in California.

1972: San Antonio's Dennis Yard surrenders a leadoff single and then does not allow another base runner, blanking Alexandria 1–0.

2001: El Paso left fielder Mike Rose and Round Rock left fielder Jason Lane both walk five times in the Express's 9–7 victory in eleven innings.

2007: San Antonio catcher Nick Hundley posts his second two-homer, five-RBI performance in a week against Tulsa, leading the Missions to an 8–3 victory.

JULY 6

1918: The Texas League season ends prematurely because of the government's "work or fight" order, which mandated that all able-bodied men must either be in the military or working in a defense-related industry.

1931: Beaumont sets a league record with six triples in a 19–3 victory over San Antonio.

1968: Albuquerque's Bill Sudakis hits two home runs and drives in eight as the Dodgers rout San Antonio 13–3. After hitting .294 and driving in seventy-five runs in 113 games in the Texas League, Sudakis finished the season with 24 games in the Majors, driving in twelve runs.

1972: Dennis James of El Paso strikes out 19 in a 12–5 triumph over Memphis, one short of a sixty-three-year-old league record set by San Antonio's Willie Mitchell. James whiffed 167 in 1972, when he went 11-3 with a 1.84 ERA.

1974: Umpire Bob Rainey has to work the plate in both ends of a double-header after locking the key to the umpires' room inside.

1982: Tulsa defeats Jackson 11–7 in twenty-three innings despite leaving a record-tying twenty-seven men on base.

1989: After scoring single runs in the first inning, San Antonio and Tulsa duel for fifteen scoreless innings before Eric Mangham doubles home Jose Offerman. Missions reliever Tim Scott picked up the victory; oddly, Scott also was the winner in San Antonio's sixteen-inning victory on May 17 at Jackson.

JULY 7

1895: Austin, with sixteen errors, and San Antonio, with eight, combine for a league record for errors in a nine-inning game.

1909: Houston's Johnny Blakeney throws a wild no-hitter against Waco, winning 4–1 despite walking eight and hitting two more.

1910: San Antonio outfielder Otto McIver gives his club a 4–3 victory by hitting a solo homer in the top of the seventeenth against Galveston. San Antonio's Brown Rogers pitched all seventeen innings, three times battling out of bases-loaded, one-out jams.

1914: San Antonio owner Morris Block turns down an offer of $5,000 from the rest of the league's owners to shut down his team for the rest of the season. The league was trying to save money on railroad fares and get down to six teams since it also was trying to get the Austin club to fold. San Antonio finished the season at 46-103 and Austin at a record-worst 31-114.

1917: Dallas's Snipe Conley wins his nineteenth game in a row, defeating Waco 5–4 in ten innings.

1942: Doyle Lade of Shreveport pitches a no-hitter against San Antonio, winning 1–0 on his own sixth-inning home run. Lade walked two and struck out three in the seven-inning contest and went on to go 18-7 with a 1.81 ERA.

1960: Newly acquired starter Gerald Glynn becomes the first right-hander to start a game for Austin in three weeks. In the previous twenty games, Austin manager Al Monchak had rotated lefties Charlie Gorin, Hank Hemmerly, Bill Hamilton, Jim Grumm and Denny Lemaster.

1966: The Houston Astros beat the Texas League All-Stars 7–6 in front of 10,076 fans in Arlington. The Astros scored three runs in the bottom of the eleventh for the victory, with the deciding run scoring on a balk by Arkansas pitcher Leo Newton.

1972: Arkansas' Dave Kent leads a twenty-three-hit attack in a 16–8 rout of Midland. Kent drove in seven runs with a single, a double and two home runs.

Midland's Jim Edmonds started the 1992 season in the Texas League but was in the Majors to stay a year later. *Texas League collection.*

1974: Catcher Tony Auferio hits two of the seven triples in his eight-year pro career to help Arkansas beat Alexandria 3–2 in ten innings. The three-base hits were the first for Auferio since 1971.

1990: Dean Palmer goes five for five with two home runs and seven RBIs as Tulsa pounds Arkansas 15–5. Palmer, who had been with the Texas Rangers briefly at the end of the 1989 season, was soon promoted to Triple-A Oklahoma City. He moved to the Majors for good in 1991.

1992: Midland's Jim Edmonds hits his third homer of the game in the bottom of the ninth, lifting the Angels to a 10–9 decision over Wichita. Edmonds finished the season at Triple-A and in 1993 launched a big-league career that lasted parts of seventeen seasons and saw him make the All-Star Game four times.

2004: Tulsa's Jeff Francis strikes out 14 Arkansas batters in seven innings, winning 6–4 in his final appearance in Double-A. In seventeen appearances for the Drillers, Francis was 13-1 with a league-best 1.98 ERA. The left-hander also struck out 147 in 113.2 innings.

JULY 8

1915: Houston player-manager Pat Newnam hits an inside-the-park homer in the bottom of the sixteenth to give his club a 2–1 victory over Beaumont.

The hit, which bounced over center fielder Al Nixon's head, gave the victory to Dode Criss, who pitched every inning and beat Joe Martina, who also went the entire way.

1925: James C. "Bad News" Galloway of Waco hits home runs in three consecutive at-bats in a game with Beaumont. Galloway hit .298 in eighteen seasons in the minors and led the Texas League in doubles in 1926 with fifty-one.

1926: Fort Worth outfielder J.E. "Eddie" Moore begins a league-record string of 573 consecutive games, not missing a contest until April 30, 1930. And he was steady at the plate during the streak, hitting .329 in 1927, .306 in '28 and .335 in '29.

1931: For the first time in league history, every team participates in a night game on the same evening.

1947: A crowd of 11,833 in Houston turns out for the first Texas League All-Star Game in five years.

1949: Clarence "Hooks" Iott of Beaumont pitches a seven-inning no-hitter, beating Shreveport 2–0. Iott walked eight, including walking the bases loaded twice. The victory was his first since May 2.

1955: Houston pitcher Bill Greason makes an unassisted putout at the plate. Greason's pitch sailed over the catcher's head but hit a concrete railing and bounced right back to him as he was charging in to cover the plate. He speared the ball, dove and tagged out the runner.

1977: Arkansas center fielder Nelson Garcia begins a streak of fourteen consecutive times on base in an 8–0 win at Tulsa. He was three for four on July 8, five for five the next night and then four for five on July 10. He walked twice during the streak.

JULY 9

1935: Galveston's Eddie Cole pitches the first nine-inning perfect game in league history. Late in the game, home-plate umpire Steve Basil calls a third

In 1935, Ed Cole pitched the first nine-inning perfect game in league history. *Texas League collection.*

strike on a pitch that observers said was obviously ball four. In his game story, *Fort Worth Star Telegram* reporter Flem Hall called Basil "the umpire with a heart." The game ended on an inside-the-park homer by Maggie McGee with two out in the bottom of the ninth. Cole went 15-19 for Galveston in 1935 and won 166 games in the minors from 1931 to 1951.

1955: Dallas first baseman Bill White hits three home runs and drives in six runs to lead the Eagles to an 11–3 victory over Fort Worth. White went on to play thirteen seasons in the Majors and serve as president of the National League.

1961: The Rio Grande Valley club moves to Victoria, the last in-season franchise shift in league history.

1964: San Antonio rallies for a 14–8 victory over El Paso, taking advantage of eight walks to score nine runs. After two outs, five straight Bullets batters walked and then Aaron Pointer drove in two with a single, Joe Morgan brought in two more with a double and Leo Posada scored two more with another single. Another walk and an El Paso error produced the final San Antonio run.

1973: Midland's Jerry Tabb hits for the cycle to lead the Cubs to a 10–9 decision over Memphis. Tabb had a single double, triple and two home runs, with his second homer coming in the bottom of the eleventh for the victory. Tabb, the Cubs' first-round pick in the 1973 draft, hit .273 and drove in forty-four runs for Midland in seventy-six games in his first season as a pro.

1977: Shreveport's Don Robinson has a busy night, giving up nine hits, striking out 15 and hitting a solo homer in a 9–1 victory over Jackson. The "Caveman" struck out 106 in 118 innings in 1977 and the following spring began a Major League career that lasted fifteen seasons.

JULY 10

1895: Four different umpires work a game between Sherman and Houston. The first was replaced because of incompetence in the first inning. Two more called the game through the seventh, and then another took over in the eighth, working the game until Klondike Douglas hit a game-winning single for Sherman in the fifteenth inning.

1903: Clyde "Sis" Bateman throws a no-hitter, stifling Fort Worth 7–0 while allowing just two walks. Bateman had one of the most remarkable seasons in league history in 1903 for a club that started the season in Paris and wound up in Waco, as he led the league in hitting, home runs and triples and also was 18-15 as a pitcher, completing thirty-two of thirty-four starts.

1917: Dallas ace Snipe Conley loses to Waco 8–3, ending his winning streak at nineteen.

1940: In the first extra-inning Texas League All-Star Game, Fort Worth's Henry "Prince" Oana drives in the winning run with a double in the eleventh inning for a 7–6 North win at Fort Worth's LaGrave Field. The South's Jack Bradsher of San Antonio hit a grand slam in the seventh inning, another All-Star first.

1959: Tulsa first baseman Duke Carmel homers in three consecutive at-bats as the Oilers triumph 8–4 over San Antonio. Carmel hit twenty-three homers and drove in seventy-one runs for Tulsa in 1959 before earning a promotion to Triple-A Rochester.

1964: Hal Breeden was a big hit in his first game with Austin, hitting a game-winning homer in the twelfth to beat Tulsa 2–1 in his first appearance since a promotion from Class-A Yakima.

1972: In his first game as a professional, Rick Richardson gives San Antonio a 3–1 victory over Shreveport with a homer in the bottom of the fourteenth inning.

1979: Ron Roenicke, who would manage San Antonio to a pennant eighteen years later, has three hits (including a double and a triple) and a dazzling catch in center field as the Texas League All-Stars beat the Arkansas Travelers 11–3.

2003: A record crowd fills El Paso's Cohen Stadium to see three big-leaguers make rehab starts for the Diablos. Randy Johnson pitched the first four innings, allowing three hits and two unearned runs. Tony Wommack and Junior Spivey played all thirteen innings in the middle infield for El Paso, which wound up winning 5–4.

DRY SPELLS

The longest stretch between pennants in league history is twenty-nine years, as San Antonio went from 1968 to 1996 without a title. Technically, the city didn't have a championship team from 1965 to 1996, but the city did not have a franchise from 1965 to 1967 after the Houston Astros moved their Texas League club to Amarillo. Midland also went twenty-nine years between titles, from 1976 to 2004.

JULY 11

1914: Austin ends a league-record thirty-game losing streak with a 9–3 victory over Fort Worth. The Senators would go on to finish the season with 114 losses, a league record that still stands. Of the three dozen players who appeared for the woeful Senators in 1914, just one would go on to a long career in the Major Leagues: seventeen-year-old Ross Youngs. Youngs wound up playing for the great New York Giants teams of the early 1920s and was named to the National Baseball Hall of Fame in 1972.

Rogers Hornsby shows off his new uniform. The Hall of Famer took over as manager of the Fort Worth Cats in 1942. *Texas League collection.*

1930: Dallas third baseman Hugh Willingham hits a home run that leaves Houston's Buff Stadium and is measured later at 532 feet on the fly. Willingham hit .321 for the Steers and hit thirty-eight homers in 1930, his first year in professional ball.

1933: Tulsa puts up ten runs in the first inning on the way to a 13–4 pounding of Galveston. The Oilers hit three homers in the big inning, including a grand slam by John Stoneham. Stoneham, a .317 hitter in fourteen minor-league seasons, hit .304 for the Oilers in 1933.

1940: Dizzy Dean becomes the first player to appear in both the Major League and Texas League All-Star Games and the only one to appear in the latter after the former. Dean started the 1940 contest for the North Division, which was managed by Rogers Hornsby.

1961: Umpire Hank Stein awards Ardmore a 9–0 forfeit after fans in Monterrey lay down a barrage of firecrackers, stones and chunks of ice on the field. Stein stopped the game with two outs in the bottom of the ninth and the Rosebuds leading 3–0.

1984: Last-minute replacement Billy Beane hits a two-run homer in the bottom of the ninth to give the East an 8–7 victory in the All-Star Game. Beane, who went on to fame as a member of the Oakland A's front office, was added to the game when Tulsa's Bob Brower was promoted to Triple-A.

2002: Adrian Myers becomes the first player to hit for the cycle at San Antonio's Wolff Stadium, going four for five and driving in six runs in the Missions' 9–2 victory over Round Rock.

2010: Corpus Christi ends a sixteen-game losing streak with a 6–5 victory over Northwest Arkansas. The win was the Hooks' first in the second half.

HALL OF FAMERS

Following are Texas League players, managers or executives who have been inducted into the National Baseball Hall of Fame, along with the year(s) they were in the league:

Grover Cleveland Alexander, 1930
Roberto Alomar, 1987
Walt Alston, 1937
Sparky Anderson, 1955
Bert Blyleven, 1992
Jim Bottomley, 1921
Willard Brown, 1953–56

Paul (left) and Dizzy Dean clown around before a game. *Texas League collection.*

Steve Carlton, 1964
Dizzy Dean, 1930–31 and 1940
Dennis Eckersley, 1974
Hank Greenberg, 1931–32
Burleigh Grimes, 1937
Tony Gwynn, 1981
Chick Hafey, 1924
Whitey Herzog, 1953
Rogers Hornsby, 1940–42, 1950
Carl Hubbell, 1927–28
Willie McCovey, 1957
Joe Medwick, 1931–32, 1948
Joe Morgan, 1964
Hal Newhouser, 1939
Phil Niekro, 1961
Gaylord Perry, 1959–60
Branch Rickey, 1904–05
Brooks Robinson, 1956
Frank Robinson, 1954
Nolan Ryan, 2000–13
Ron Santo, 1959
Al Simmons, 1923
George Sisler, 1932
Duke Snider, 1946, 1967, 1972
Tris Speaker, 1906–07
Bruce Sutter, 1974–75
Don Sutton, 1965
Bill Terry, 1916–17
Earl Weaver, 1951–52
Zach Wheat, 1908
Billy Williams, 1959
Dick Williams, 1948–50, 1955
Ross Youngs, 1913–14

Hall of Famer Zach Wheat played in the Texas League in 1908. *Photo Courtesy Bain News Service Archives, Library of Congress.*

JULY 12

1942: Fort Worth's Ed Greer beats Tulsa 7–0 in just sixty-nine minutes. The game started eight minutes early, at 8:07 p.m., and fans were still outside the park buying tickets when it ended and the lights went off at 9:16 p.m.

1951: Tom Gorman of Beaumont launches a scoreless inning streak that would stretch to forty-two innings, the longest in league history. The string began with the final eight innings of a 3–2 victory over Oklahoma City and then was followed by three nine-inning shutouts. It finally ended in the eighth inning of a 2–0 loss to Tulsa.

1958: Corpus Christi, shut out 5–0 by Austin in the first game of a double-header, explodes for twenty-four hits in the 26–3 nightcap romp. The Giants scored in all but the first inning, posting ten runs in the sixth.

1959: The Mexican League All-Stars beat the Texas League Stars 9–3 in the first-ever international All-Star Game. The contest in Mexico City attracted 19,089 fans, the largest to ever see a Texas League All-Star Game.

1963: Amarillo manager Joe Macko sets a league record by using five pitchers in the ninth inning of an 8–7 victory at El Paso.

1965: For the second time in a month, Tulsa and Austin battle for fifteen innings, with Tulsa coming out on top, this time by the score of 5–4. The game featured a wild brawl that led to multiple ejections, as well as one casualty—the glasses of Austin outfielder Barry Morgan, which were stepped on during the mêlée.

1972: Shreveport's Greg Jaycox strikes out fifteen and yields just two hits in an 8–0 victory over San Antonio. Jaycox walked one batter and retired the last fifteen men he faced. The erratic right-hander won nine games between Double-A and Triple-A in 1972 and was out of baseball by the end of the 1973 season.

1980: Kelly Paris puts up four doubles and scores the winning run in the tenth inning as Arkansas takes a 10–9 decision at Amarillo. Fred Tisdale chipped in with two home runs and four RBIs in the thirty-one-hit slugfest.

JULY 13

1895: Sherman ends a sixteen-game winning streak by Galveston pitcher George Bristow, winning 3–2. Bristow appeared in a league-high forty-eight games in 1895, the second of his twelve seasons in baseball.

1904: Jack Huffmeister of Dallas allows only one hit in eleven innings but loses 6–5 to Fort Worth, thanks to a league-record sixteen errors behind him.

1934: A thirteen-inning duel between San Antonio and Tulsa ends at 10-all after a dust storm blows into Tulsa. A ninth-inning, two-run homer by the Missions' catcher Sam Harshaney tied the game at 9 and sent it into extra innings. Both clubs scored in the twelfth before the dust storm arrived.

1934: Oklahoma City scores eleven runs on just six hits in the first inning on the way to a 20–11 victory over Galveston. The Indians wound up with twelve walks and fifteen hits, led by Tank Horton, who went four for five.

1977: Juan Berenguer leads Jackson to a 2–2 win over El Paso with a two-hit, sixteen-strikeout performance. Jackson won in the bottom of the ninth using a hit, a stolen base, a walk and three El Paso errors. "Senor Smoke" played fifteen seasons in the Major Leagues and won a career-high eleven games for the world champion Detroit Tigers in 1984.

1991: Four San Antonio pitchers combine to shut out Arkansas in both halves of a double-header. Mike Wilkins, the winner in the second game, also had two doubles and three RBIs.

JULY 14

1897: Paris rolls over Houston 20–0 in a game shortened to five innings to allow the Buffs to slink out of town on a train to Waco. The Midlands had twenty-one hits, including five doubles, three triples and three home runs.

1919: San Antonio explodes for ten runs in the top of the twelfth inning to shock Dallas 15–5. The outburst was the first double-digit extra inning in league history—and it wouldn't be duplicated for nearly eighty years, until

San Antonio scored eleven against Wichita in the eleventh inning on August 19, 1998.

1930: San Antonio's Sam Leslie drives in eight runs with two doubles and two homers in a 12–10 victory at Fort Worth. Leslie hit .409 in 73 games for the Missions and .392 overall in 1930. The Mississippi native wound up playing in 822 games in ten seasons in the Majors.

1947: Houston pitcher Clarence Beers stifles Tulsa on the mound and also drives in all six of his team's runs with a two-run double, a three-run double and a sacrifice fly. Beers went on to lead the league with twenty-five victories.

1952: Johnny Vander Meer of Tulsa pitches a no-hitter against Beaumont just over fourteen years after his back-to-back no-hitters in the Major Leagues. Vander Meer, thirty-seven, would pitch three more seasons in the minors.

1956: Despite a telegram from league president Dick Butler, Louisiana governor Earl Long signs a bill banning athletic competition between black and white players. Shreveport drops out of the league after the 1957 season and does not return until 1968.

1961: Larry Maxie becomes the second of three Texas League pitchers to throw two no-hitters in a season, beating Poza Rica 5–0. The twenty-year-old Maxie had thrown a 2–0 no-hitter on June 14 at Victoria. Fort Worth's Alex Dupree threw two no-hitters in 1906 and Bud Smith two in 2000.

1988: San Antonio and Jackson begin play on what was to become the longest game in league history and the longest scoreless game in baseball. After twenty-five innings of a scoreless tie, the game was suspended at 2:29 a.m. Two days later, the game was completed, with San Antonio winning 1–0 in the twenty-sixth inning.

1998: Tulsa's Ruben Mateo's hitting streak ends at 27 games. Mateo was 51 for 126 in those games and hit .309 in 107 games with the Drillers in 1998. Mateo made his Major League debut for the Texas Rangers the following year.

JULY 15

1908: Austin's Walter Sullivan throws a no-hitter against Waco, winning 7–0. Sullivan had been traded to Austin by Waco earlier in the season. The only two base runners for Waco reached via errors.

1916: In the second game of a double-header, "Sergeant" Clyde Barfoot helps Galveston complete a sweep with a seven-inning no-hitter. Barfoot was in the third of nine Texas League seasons that would see him go 120-100.

1930: Wichita Falls and Houston combine for thirty-five runs and forty hits in a game won by the Spudders, 21–14. Houston center fielder Oliver Hunt drove in seven runs, and Wichita Falls' Jack Kloza was four for five with six RBIs.

1936: In the second game of a double-header, Oklahoma City's Sig Jakucki pitches a seven-inning no-hitter against the Galveston Buccaneers, winning 10–0. Galveston's Orville Armbrust had limited the Indians to a single hit in the first game. The series included two no-hitters and a one-hitter.

1961: Ardmore's Don MacLeod pitches a one-hitter and scores the only run of the game in a 1–0 decision over Veracruz. The only hit surrendered by the Canadian right-hander was an opposite-field single by Ernest Garcia in the eighth inning.

1963: Tulsa's Ed Spiezio collects a single, a double, two home runs and eight RBIs by the fifth inning of a 16–2 victory over El Paso. Spiezio came up with men in scoring position in the sixth and eighth innings but could not add to his total. Spiezio played nine seasons in the Major Leagues, from 1964 to 1972, and his son, Scott, appeared in twelve, from 1996 to 2007.

1966: All four Texas League games are decided by the score of 2–1. Austin and El Paso split a double-header, while Albuquerque topped Dallas–Fort Worth and Amarillo got by Arkansas.

JULY 16

1934: The Galveston Buccaneers sell outfielder Roy "Beau" Bell to the St. Louis Browns for $17,500. Bell, Texas A&M's first All-American in any sport, went on to play seven seasons in the big leagues.

1937: Houston pitcher John Grodzicki strikes out six batters in a row in the Texas League All-Star Game, starting with the league's leading hitter, Homer Peel, whose average going into the game was .401. He then fanned Red Harvel, Joe Bilgere, Lou Brower, Norman McCaskill and Ed Greer.

1951: Shreveport gets eight straight hits to open the game against Oklahoma City and winds up scoring seven runs in the first inning. The Sports went on to win 9–6.

1964: Left-hander Nick DeMatteis holds Tulsa hitless as he leads El Paso over the Drillers 1–0. DeMatteis, a converted outfielder, went 9-12 for the Sun Kings in 1964, striking out 142 in 180 innings.

1967: Five errors, two walks and five hits led to ten runs for Amarillo in the eighth inning of a 17–0 pounding of Austin.

1976: John Poloni breaks a San Antonio club record, winning his ninth straight game with a 1–0 shutout of Lafayette. He broke Dennis Eckersley's record from 1974. However, Poloni appeared in just two games in the Major Leagues; Eckersley played twenty-four seasons and was named to the National Baseball Hall of Fame in 2004.

1978: Tulsa's Dave Righetti strikes out 21 Midland Cubs in nine innings, breaking a sixty-nine-year-old league record. However, the nineteen-year-old does not get a decision, as he was pulled from the game in the ninth with the score tied at two. Righetti struck out 127 batters in ninety-one innings in his only season in the Texas League.

San Antonio slugger Michael Morse in 2004. *Photo by Christie L. Cathey.*

1980: Arkansas scores ten times in the ninth inning to finish off a 19–3 romp over San Antonio. Fred Tisdale and Nelson Garcia each had three hits and four RBIs in the game. The Travelers, who sent thirteen men to the plate in the ninth, also batted around in the second and fifth innings.

2004: Newly acquired Michael Morse drives in five runs with a sacrifice fly and a grand slam and eighteen-year-old Felix Hernandez wins his first game in Double-A as San Antonio rips Round Rock 11–3. Hernandez finished the season 14-4 with 172 strikeouts in 149.1 innings in Class A and Double-A, and by the end of 2005, he was in the Major Leagues to stay.

FUTURE FAME

Four players who have been named the Texas League player of the year or pitcher of the year have gone on to earn a spot in the National Baseball Hall of Fame: Dizzy Dean, who was the first Texas League honoree in 1931; Hank Greenberg, who won the honor in 1932; Joe Morgan, who took it in 1964; and Dennis Eckersley, who was honored in 1974.

JULY 17

1922: Houston forfeits a game at San Antonio—while leading 4–0. Houston pitcher Bill Bailey was ejected for disputing a ball-four call by plate umpire Jack Daly. Buffs skipper George Whiteman insisted that his new pitcher be given at least twenty-five warm-up pitches. Daly refused, and Whiteman refused to bring in a pitcher, so the game was awarded to the Bears.

1932: Zeke Bonura caps a seven-RBI day with a two-run double in the bottom of the ninth that gives his team a 9–8 victory over Beaumont. Bonura hit .322 with twenty-one homers in 1932 and jumped to .357 with twenty-four home runs for the Steers in 1933.

1993: Todd Hollandsworth gives San Antonio a 1–0 victory over Arkansas with a homer leading off the bottom of the eleventh inning. It was Hollandsworth's first at-bat of the game after entering as a defensive replacement.

1998: Tyrone Horne, Mike Hardge and Chris Richards combine for eight hits and fifteen RBIs as Arkansas pounds Wichita 18–6. Center fielder J.D. Drew went two for two with four walks and also scored five times.

JULY 18

1919: Gus Bono of Shreveport, released by two different teams earlier in the season, pitches a 2–1 no-hitter against San Antonio. Bono's gem came three weeks after he was released by Waco. He had started the season with Dallas but had been let go early in the season and signed by Waco.

1930: The first league game to finish after midnight ends when Shreveport catcher Adolph Krauss homers in the bottom of the fifteenth to give the Sports a 7–6 win over Beaumont.

Tulsa's Jim Beauchamp hit .337 and drove in 105 runs in 1963. *Texas League collection.*

1934: Texas League veteran umpire Ziggy Sears's contract is sold to the National League. He is the fourth TL umpire to go directly to the Majors.

1939: Houston's Ernie White pitches a no-hitter against Fort Worth, winning 2–0. White won fifteen games and had a stellar 2.62 ERA for the Buffs in 1939.

1963: Jim Beauchamp hits for the cycle to lead Tulsa over El Paso 14–5. His single, double, triple and two home runs drove in a total of 7 runs. Beauchamp hit .337 and drove in 105 runs for the Oilers in 1963.

1971: A ten-inning victory for San Antonio over Arkansas is reversed when league president Bobby Bragan upholds a protest by Travelers manager Jack Krol in the ninth inning. Bragan said a rulebook error by the umpire allowed San Antonio to take a 3–2 lead in the ninth, so the game went into the books as a 2–2 tie with stats counting up to the point of the protest.

JULY 19

1930: Dallas takes the wild first game of a double-header from Wichita Falls, winning 13–12 in thirteen innings. The teams were tied at 7 after the regulation seven innings and then both scored twice in the twelfth. The Steers scored five times in the top of the thirteenth; the Spudders came back in the bottom with four and left the bases loaded. The teams played to a 5–5 tie in the nightcap, which was called because of darkness.

1934: Right fielder Stanley Schino of Dallas goes five for five for the second straight day as the Eagles beat San Antonio 10–3. Schino, who hit .314 in fifty-two games for Dallas in 1934, drove in eleven runs in the two games.

1936: Beaumont's Frank "Dingle" Croucher walks, ending a record streak of forty-five games without a free pass.

1957: Dallas's Willie McCovey ties a league record when he rips three triples in a 7–3 victory over Shreveport. McCovey went on to make his big-league debut in 1959, and he was named to the National Baseball Hall of Fame in 1986.

1961: San Antonio gets triples from Ralph Holding, Nelson Mathews and Elder White in a three-run third inning, helping the Missions top Veracruz 5–4. It was the only time in league history a club recorded three triples in the same inning. Matthews wound up tying for the league lead in three-baggers with ten in 1961.

1974: In one of the most lopsided shutouts in league history, Shreveport pounds Midland 21–0. Sam Mejias led the Captains' twenty-seven-hit attack as he went five for seven, including a grand slam in the fourth inning. George Vasquez went four for six with two home runs and a double. Tom Stedman and Dave Lindsey also had four hits each.

1991: Damion Easley drives in six runs with a three-for-four night as Midland pounds Shreveport 12–4. The winning pitcher for the Angels was Fernando Valenzuela, who allowed just one run on three hits in six innings. A total of 6,788 fans, a record for Angels Stadium, were on hand to see Valenzuela, who was making his final rehabilitation start before returning to the Major Leagues.

1993: Wichita outfielder Dwayne Hosey hits two solo home runs in the Texas League All-Star Game to win the MVP award and then almost decides the outcome of the tied game in a home-run contest.

1998: Mike Groppuso produces all the offense El Paso needs in a 4–3 victory at Shreveport. He went three for four with a double, a triple and a home run, driving in all four runs. Groppuso hit .300 and drove in ninety runs for the Diablos in 1998, a year after being signed by the parent Brewers from the Rio Grande Valley Whitewings of the independent Texas-Louisiana League.

2011: Northwest Arkansas turned the first triple play and posted the first no-hitter in franchise history on the same night, nipping Arkansas 1–0. Will Smith and Kelvin Herrera held the Travelers hitless, and the Naturals turned an around-the-horn triple play in the sixth after back-to-back walks.

July 20

1924: Shortly after Dallas's 3–0 victory over Beaumont, a fire breaks out near the clubhouse at Steers Park. Some players had to flee the building half-clothed, and in the end, the park and all its contents, two nearby houses and several vehicles were destroyed—a total loss of $60,000. Dallas wound up finishing the season at the home of the Dallas Black Giants, and the club played for several days in uniforms borrowed from Wichita Falls.

1937: John Grodzicki strikes out eleven and hits a solo homer to lead the Houston Buffs to a 1–0 victory over Tulsa. Grodzicki won eighteen games for the Buffs in 1937, a career high.

1940: Beaumont gets nine straight hits and puts thirteen straight on base in the third inning of an 11–9 victory over the San Antonio Missions. Beaumont broke three records in the inning: nine consecutive hits, thirteen consecutive runners on base and nine singles. The latter two records still stand.

1968: Jim Britton and James Sanders, just promoted from Magic Valley in the rookie-level Pioneer League, team up to throw a 1–0 no-hitter for Shreveport against San Antonio.

1968: Albuquerque manager Roger Craig makes twenty-three defensive shifts in a 4–1 loss to Memphis. After outfielder Von Joshua is hurt in the fourth, Craig moves him to first base and then uses pitcher Dick Dare to pinch hit for him in the fifth. From then on, Dare is moved eight times, Kenny Washington four times and Henry Williams, the starting and losing pitcher, six times.

1983: The West All-Stars pound out ten hits on the way to a 10–4 decision at El Paso. San Antonio's Sid Fernandez struck out seven batters in his four innings of work, the best total ever in a Texas League All-Star Game. Fernandez went on to win the league's pitching Triple Crown, leading the league in victories (thirteen), ERA (2.82) and strikeouts (209).

1992: Designated hitter Adell Davenport of Shreveport hits a three-run homer with two out in the bottom of the ninth inning, highlighting a seven-run inning that gave the East an 8–6 victory in the Texas League All-Star Game at Jackson.

JULY 21

1892: A crowd of more than one thousand pays fifty cents each to attend a night exhibition game between Houston and Galveston. Proceeds went to ensure that both clubs would have enough money to finish the season.

1930: Hugh Willingham collects five RBIs with a pair of homers to power Dallas past Houston 10–6 in the first night game at Buffs Stadium. More than twelve thousand fans attend the game, while several thousand more watch from vantage points outside the stadium.

1939: Thanks to a bases-loaded walk and a thunderstorm, Tulsa beats Oklahoma City 1–0 without a hit. After Oklahoma City starter Orval Grove walked the bases loaded with two out in the fifth, player-manager Wilcy Moore came in to relieve him and walked in a run. Moments after the third out of the inning, a storm knocked out the lights, and the game was called.

1950: Houston and Dallas battle for nineteen innings and over four hours to a 1–1 tie, as the game ends at a midnight curfew. Dallas starter Bob Malloy went the first fourteen innings, and Houston starter Fred McGaha pitched the first twelve.

1951: St. Louis Browns owner Bill Veeck and his general manager, Rudy Schaeffer, announce they have sold their stock in the Oklahoma City Indians. Veeck retained his ownership of the San Antonio Missions.

1970: Mike Floyd goes four for four—all doubles—leading El Paso over Arkansas 9–5. Floyd finished the season with twenty-four doubles, a career high.

1971: Arkansas and Dallas–Fort Worth combine to leave fifty runners on base in a twenty-two-inning, six-hour duel. The Travelers won 5–4 at 1:26 a.m.

2004: Ian Kinsler and Jason Botts both crush grand slams for Frisco in a 15–6 victory over San Antonio. Botts, who had another homer and a double in the game, wound up with seven RBIs.

July 22

1892: San Antonio and Waco join the Texas League, replacing Dallas and Fort Worth, which dropped out on July 8. Playing each other at Waco in their league debuts, Waco pounded San Antonio 14–6.

1906: Cleburne and Fort Worth play to a nineteen-inning scoreless tie that ends only when it becomes too dark to see. Cleburne starter Walter "Hickory" Dickson gave up just six hits and walked only two, while Alex Dupree of Fort Worth allowed nine hits and did not walk a man. A player from each team umpired the entire contest since the regularly scheduled umpire was not available.

1907: Trapper Longley of Temple goes seven for seven in a game against Galveston. The contest was the highlight of an eleven-season pro career for Longley, a .274 hitter.

1907: Austin sets a pro baseball record that is still unbroken by stealing twenty-three bases in a 44–0 win over San Antonio. San Antonio had lost the first game of a double-header, forfeiting the contest to Austin after repeated run-ins with umpire Jack Schuster. Playing the second game only to avoid a league fine, San Antonio made a farce of the proceedings by dropping fly balls, refusing to handle grounders and putting players in and out of the game without notice.

1914: Despite three errors and five walks, San Antonio's George Crable throws a no-hitter against the Dallas Giants, winning 2–1. San Antonio scored the winning run in the bottom of the ninth on a single by Everitt Sheffield. Crable won a career-high seventeen games for the Bronchos in 1914.

1933: Tulsa left-hander Spades Wood collects his first victory of the season with a 9–2 no-hitter against Houston. Both of the Buffs' runs came in the sixth inning, when Wood walked five batters. He won just one other game in 1933 and lost a total of eleven.

1961: Don MacLeod tosses his second consecutive shutout for Ardmore, shackling Mexico City on two hits and winning 6–0 in a game shortened to six innings by rain. In his previous outing, MacLeod beat Veracruz 1–0 on one hit.

1964: Albuquerque unleashes twenty-two hits, seven of which are home runs, as the Dukes pound El Paso 23–3. Paul Jernigan had seven RBIs, thanks to a bases-loaded triple and a grand slam.

1968: Steve Renko of Memphis strikes out thirteen Albuquerque hitters on the way to a 1–0 no-hitter. Renko's masterpiece was the seventh no-hitter of the 1968 season, the most since eight were thrown in 1906.

1985: El Paso beats Tulsa 7–2 at the home ballpark of the Drillers' parent club, Arlington Stadium. The Diablos defeated the Rangers' top pitching prospect, Bobby Witt, who walked seven and struck out seven in six innings.

1993: San Antonio's Todd Hollandsworth drives in seven runs with a pair of three-run homers and a sacrifice fly, leading the Missions to an 11–2 pounding of Tulsa. Hollandsworth, the National League Rookie of the Year in 1996, played twelve seasons in the Major Leagues.

2007: Tulsa first-base coach Mike Coolbaugh dies after being struck by a line drive off the bat of the Drillers' Tino Sanchez. Coolbaugh had been with the Drillers just three weeks, joining the club as hitting coach after playing seventeen seasons of pro ball from 1990 to 2006.

Mike Coolbaugh was struck and killed by a line drive while coaching first base for the Tulsa Drillers in 2007. *Photo by Jim Vasaldua.*

July 23

1910: Gene Dale of Dallas beats Houston 6–1 with a no-hitter; the Buffs' run came as the result of four consecutive walks in the sixth.

1930: Adolph Krauss singles home the deciding run in the top of the tenth as Shreveport wins the first night game in San Antonio, 2–1. The Indians were the fourth Texas League team to install lights.

1950: Three Beaumont runners score on a strikeout during a bizarre ten-run inning against Tulsa. With the bases loaded, Beaumont catcher Walt Wrona let strike three get past him. Two runners scored as he was looking for the ball, and another came home when he finally found the ball but threw wildly back to home. The Oilers were charged with a league-record six errors in the inning.

1952: Shreveport, which had been in last place on July 1, defeats Dallas 8–1 to take over the league lead. The Sports fell back to third place by the end of the regular season but went on to win the championship series in five games over Oklahoma City.

1953: Optioned to Tulsa after disappointing performances at Cincinnati and Indianapolis, pitcher Howie Judson begins a streak that sees him go 11-0 in ten starts and four relief appearances.

1953: San Antonio's Ryne Duren throws a one-hitter in the nine-inning nightcap of a double-header at Tulsa but loses 2–0, thanks to ten walks and three hit batsmen. Tulsa used three walks, a hit batter and its lone single, by shortstop Ziggy Jasiniski, to score two runs in the fourth inning.

1964: For the second time in four games, San Antonio's Aaron Pointer ends a game with a home run, this one a two-out, pinch-hit, three-run shot in a 5–4 victory over Austin. Pointer had beaten Albuquerque three days earlier with a three-run homer in the eleventh inning.

1995: Jackson third baseman Tim Forkner drives in seven runs with two singles and two home runs to lead the Generals to a 16–5 romp over El Paso.

1999: San Antonio scores nine runs in the bottom of the ninth to edge Tulsa 15–14. The Missions' Tony Mota doubled twice in the inning to tie a league record. San Antonio had just thirteen hits but benefited from twelve walks.

JULY 24

1936: The Texas League plays its first All-Star Game, with teams representing the North and South divisions selected by vote of the fans. A crowd of 9,050 in Dallas saw the South edge the North 4–2.

1953: Fort Worth third baseman Jim Baxes commits an error, ending a league-record string of 123 errorless chances. In 3,756 chances in nine minor-league seasons, Baxes committed just 208 errors.

1954: The wind helps Houston pull off a triple play at Tulsa. In the third inning, with men on first and second, Ted Tappe crushed a ball deep to left field. But the wind held it up, and Vince Moreci caught it at the fence. Joe Szekely was easily doubled off first. Jim Bolger, who had forgotten how many men were out, wandered off second base and was tagged out.

1967: El Paso catcher Tom Egan drives in nine runs in the Sun Kings' 13–3 pounding of Arkansas. The twenty-one-year-old Egan hit three-run home runs in the first and fifth, a two-run single in the sixth and a run-scoring infield hit in the eighth.

1986: Shreveport's Jeff Brantley strikes out seventeen and does not allow a hit until the ninth inning in an 8–4 decision over Midland. Brantley made it to the Major Leagues two years later and wound up appearing in 615 games from 1988 to 2001. Brantley led the National League with forty-four saves in 1996.

1991: San Antonio's Pedro Martinez outduels Arkansas' Donavan Osborne, winning 1–0. Martinez limited the Travelers to two hits and struck out nine. Osborne gave up three hits and two walks and struck out eight. The Missions' run came in the sixth when Eric Young scored on a single by Raul Mondesi.

1994: Arkansas right-hander Brian Barber strikes out 14 San Antonio batters in 7 innings as the Travelers beat the Missions 5–2. Between Double-A and Triple-A, Barber struck out 149 batters in 121.1 innings in 1994.

2006: The league's teams tie a 104-year-old record by hitting a combined twenty-one homers in one night. Arkansas and Springfield had nine between them, Tulsa and Wichita hit seven, San Antonio and Round Rock combined for three and Midland and Frisco had one. The last time the league hit twenty-one homers in one day was when Corsicana hit twenty-one in the famous 51–3 victory over Texarkana on June 15, 1902.

2006: Midland scores six runs after two outs in the bottom of the ninth to force extra innings. The RockHounds then got a two-out RBI single from Kurt Suzuki in the thirteenth to win 10–9.

2013: All four regularly scheduled Texas League games end in shutouts, as Northwest Arkansas beats Arkansas 7–0, Midland tops Frisco 6–0, Corpus

Christi blanks San Antonio 5–0 and Tulsa edges Springfield 3–0. Northwest Arkansas outslugged Arkansas 11–8 in a makeup game.

JULY 25

1914: For the second time in a month, Houston steals fifteen bases against Austin in a 17–6 romp. Houston center fielder Johnny Frierson led the way with six, including a steal of home in the first inning.

1923: San Antonio's Ike Boone extends his hitting streak to thirty-four games, a record that would stand until 1969.

1937: Claude Horton of Dallas walks fourteen but still beats San Antonio, 14–5. Horton held the Missions to just six hits.

1975: El Paso's Paul Dade goes five for six with eight RBIs in the Diablos' 20–10 victory over San Antonio. Dade clubbed a two-run home run in the second, a three-run shot in the fourth, a run-scoring single in the fifth and a two-run double in the eighth. Dade, the California Angels' first-round draft pick in 1970, hit .332 in one hundred games with El Paso in 1975.

1982: In his second game in the Texas League, Amarillo outfielder Kevin McReynolds leads the Gold Sox to a 7–4, ten-inning victory over Arkansas. McReynolds drove in all his club's runs with a sixth-inning triple, a three-run home run in the eighth that sent the game to extra innings and another three-run shot in the tenth.

2013: Springfield and Northwest Arkansas pitchers combine for a league-record thirty-two strikeouts in the Naturals' 6–0 victory. Naturals pitchers whiffed eighteen and Springfield's fourteen.

JULY 26

1895: Houston pitcher Irwin Isaacs gives up twenty-eight hits and walks eight as the Mud Cats fall to Dallas 31–1. Houston also committed fifteen errors. Ed Ashenback went six for seven for Dallas.

1907: Ivy Tevis throws a one-hitter against San Antonio in the first game of a double-header and a three-hitter in the second game, winning 1–0 and 8–0. The only hit Tevis allowed in the first game came with two outs in the first inning, and San Antonio did not collect another hit until the eighth inning of the nightcap.

1958: Two policemen summoned by umpire Bill Valentine remove Houston manager Harry Walker from the ballpark following a first-inning ejection.

1977: Tulsa's Danny Darwin strikes out twelve batters for his second start in a row. The "Bonham Bullet" finished the season 13-4 with a 2.51 ERA and pitched in the Majors from 1978 to 1998.

JULY 27

1888: A wild bull charges Austin outfielders during a home game, ending the contest prematurely.

1909: Dallas's Rube Peters beats Waco 2–0 with a no-hitter. Peters was a twenty-four-game winner for the Giants in 1908.

1921: Houston's Clyde Barfoot stops Wichita Falls' Tex McDonald's streak of eleven hits in eleven at-bats. The streak, which included seven singles, two doubles and two home runs, set a league record that stood until 1937, when Tulsa's Tony York collected twelve hits in twelve at-bats. York's mark still stands.

1922: Kedzi Kirkham of San Antonio has his hitting streak snapped at thirty-two. Kirkham was no stranger to streaks, having once collected thirty-two hits in thirty-nine at-bats for St. Joseph in the Western League.

1922: In a game that featured thirty-five hits, seventeen walks and eight errors, Wichita Falls outlasts Houston 15–14, scoring two runs in the bottom of the ninth inning. Pitcher Adolph Ruth won the game with a looping, one-out single behind second base.

1938: Houston's Mort Cooper strikes out 14 Fort Worth batters during a six-hit, 6–0 victory over the Panthers. Cooper wound up leading the league in strikeouts with 201 in 202 innings.

1955: Beaumont sends nineteen men to the plate in the third inning, scoring thirteen runs on the way to a 21–16 victory at Tulsa. The first ten men who came to the plate scored.

1960: In front of a crowd of 10,023, the St. Louis Cardinals beat Tulsa 12–5 despite home runs from Tulsa's Artie Burnett, Jim Hickman and Jim Beauchamp. Hitting leaders for the Cards were future National League president Bill White, Julian Javier and Curt Flood. Walt Moryn had a homer, and Stan Musial was one for one with a walk and a run scored.

1998: Arkansas' Tyrone Horne hits for the "homer cycle" in San Antonio, with a solo shot in the fifth inning, a two-run blast in the first, a three-run knock in the sixth and a grand slam in the second. He finishes four for five with ten RBIs and receives a standing ovation from Missions fans when he strikes out in his final at-bat.

2003: Midland's Adam Morrisey hits two homers off fellow Australian and San Antonio ace Travis Blackley. The RockHounds' second baseman also drove in the tying run in the ninth and the game-winning run in the tenth in a 5–4 decision over the Missions.

Arkansas' Tyrone Horne hit for the "homer cycle" in 1998. *Photo by Jim Vasaldua.*

RBI MACHINES

A total of seven players have driven in ten or more runs in a Texas League game, most recently Midland's Tommy Everidge in 2008. Jay Clarke's sixteen is the league record, set in 1902 in Corsicana's 51–3 destruction of Texarkana.

JULY 28

1923: Houston's Bill Bailey loses his sixteenth consecutive game, tying a league record. The left-hander had little luck, though, as half the losses were decided by one run and four were in extra innings. He and Floyd Kroh, who lost sixteen in a row for three teams in 1920, share the dubious honor.

1937: Fort Worth right-hander Ed Greer no-hits Houston but loses 1–0. Greer, who played in the minors from 1923 to 1946 and won 295 games, was the league's ERA champion in 1939 (2.28) when he won twenty-two games.

1953: Dallas's Howard Anderson pitches a 5–0 no-hitter against San Antonio. Anderson walked seven but struck out nine in the double-header opener. Anderson was a thirteen-game winner in 1953 with a 3.35 ERA.

1959: Tulsa center fielder Jim Hickman leads the Oilers to a 6–3 victory over Monterrey, hitting a two-run homer in the third inning, throwing out a runner at the plate to preserve a 3–3 tie and then hitting a three-run homer in the tenth. "Gentleman Jim" went on to play thirteen seasons in the Major Leagues and was selected to the All-Star Game in 1970 as a member of the Chicago Cubs.

1964: San Antonio and Fort Worth play with two baseballs at a time—just for a few minutes. Ball four to the Bullets' Von McDaniel got loose and rolled all the way to the backstop. But umpire Hank DiJohnson didn't see it, and he handed a new one to Fort Worth catcher John Felske. Felske threw it to pitcher Billy Connors, who threw to second base in time to catch McDaniel. After much discussion and a protest from San Antonio, McDaniel was sent back to first base.

1966: Pitcher Joe Niekro makes an impressive Texas League debut, leading Dallas–Fort Worth to a four-hit, 5–0 win over Amarillo. Niekro also hit a two-run homer in his first game since joining the Spurs from Class-A Quincy.

1972: Memphis's Lazaro del Orbe makes up for three late-inning errors with a bases-loaded single in the fourteenth inning that gives the Blues a 4–2 victory over San Antonio.

1990: San Antonio collects just one hit all day and still tops Arkansas 2–1. The Missions scored their runs on an error, a stolen base, a walk, a single, a wild pitch and a sacrifice bunt in the eighth inning.

2005: Frisco pitchers A.J. Murray, Steve Karsay and Scott Feldman combine to throw the third nine-inning perfect game in league history, beating Corpus Christi 3–0. There have also been two perfect games of fewer than nine innings: Al Shealy of Tulsa pitched one against San Antonio in 1935 in a seven-inning nightcap to a double-header, and Martin Perez of Tulsa threw one in 2011 in a five-inning game shortened by rain.

Frisco pitcher A.J. Murray was part of a trio that threw a perfect game against Corpus Christi in 2005. *Texas League collection.*

2008: Midland's Jeremy Brown hits into the team's record-tying third triple play of the season, matching a mark set by the 1923 Fort Worth Cats. Brown was the final out in all three of the triple plays in 2008.

2008: Arkansas' Mark Trumbo goes five for five with two homers and a double in his Double-A debut, leading the Travelers past Tulsa 12–5.

JULY 29

Branch Rickey was a moderately successful player in the Texas League, but he went on to be a pioneer as an executive. *Photo Courtesy Bain News Service Archives, Library of Congress.*

1897: Led by Jake Gettman's seven-for-seven day, Fort Worth pounds Dallas 34–13. Gettman, who would go on to lead the league in runs scored, crossed the plate seven times.

1904: Second baseman George Andreas and catcher Branch Rickey each collect four hits as Dallas pounds Corsicana pitcher Monte Method for twenty-five hits, winning 16–3. Andreas also stole five bases.

1908: Ivy Tevis of Houston faces just twenty-eight batters in his 1–0, no-hit win over Waco. Tevis walked one batter and struck out nine. Waco's Pep Hornsby, brother of future hitting great Rogers Hornsby, was nearly as good, holding Houston to four hits, but his error in the eighth led to the game's only run. Tevis won fifty-three games in four seasons in the Texas League, including a league-high twenty-four in 1907.

1924: Led by catcher George Bischoff, who was four for five with a homer and a double, Fort Worth routs Galveston 17–2. Bischoff's biggest hit was an inside-the-park home run in Fort Worth's seven-run third inning. Bischoff came all the way around after left fielder George Whiteman overran his fly ball, allowing it to roll to the fence.

1930: Fort Worth's Lil Stoner strikes out eighteen San Antonio hitters en route to a 5–1 victory. Stoner walked five but allowed just two hits.

1946: Tulsa beats Houston 10–7 with two inside-the-park home runs. Wilmer Skeen came around in the first after his sinking liner got past Houston center fielder Jim Basso. Jack Richards duplicated the feat in the three-run seventh when his liner bounced over Basso's head.

1966: Arkansas shuts out Austin for the third day in a row, winning behind the three-hit pitching of Fred Wall. The Travelers dominated the Braves the entire season, shutting them out nine times, but Austin had its revenge, beating Arkansas in a league championship series shortened to one game because of rain.

1976: San Antonio scores two runs when Alexandria catcher Rick Bradley throws away a potential double-play ball. The Missions escaped with an 11–9 victory in fifteen innings.

1976: Craig Stimac makes a big impression in his debut for Amarillo, hitting homers in his first two at-bats after his promotion from the Class-A California League. In his next thirty games for the Gold Sox, Stimac added just one more home run.

2011: Frisco right-hander Joe Wieland throws the first solo nine-inning no-hitter in team history, blanking San Antonio 3–0. The only runner to reach base did so on a walk and was wiped out in a double play. Ironically, Wieland joined San Antonio days later when he was involved in a trade-deadline deal between the Texas Rangers and San Diego Padres.

POWER CATS

Fort Worth ruled the Texas League from 1920 to 1925, claiming six straight pennants, and also claimed the postseason Dixie Series against the Southern Association champions five out of six times. The 1924 Panthers might have been the best of the best, winning 109 games and finishing an incredible 30½ games ahead of second-place Houston. At 109-40, the Cats also had the best winning percentage in league history.

JULY 30

1905: Pitching under a pseudonym because he did not like to play on Sundays, Dallas's Harry Ables beats Fort Worth in both ends of a double-header. Ables gave up just five hits all day, one in the first contest. The sweep wrapped up a week that saw the left-hander give up just three runs in five appearances.

1907: Austin pitchers begin a streak of seven shutouts in nine days, including five in a row. Rube Sutor and Parson McGill each posted two shutouts during the streak.

1940: Loy Hanning of San Antonio comes within a walk of a perfect game, beating Tulsa 4–0 in the nightcap of a double-header. Hanning struck out twelve.

1952: Bill Greason becomes the second African American player in the Texas League, leading Oklahoma City to a 6–4 victory over Shreveport. Greason would go on to post a 9-1 record with a 2.14 ERA in ten starts for the Indians.

1956: San Antonio and Shreveport trade blowouts in a double-header at San Antonio. In the opener, second baseman Jack Hollis went four for four with three doubles in the Sports' 13–3 victory. In the second game, the Missions' Dave Roberts drove in six runs with a double and three singles as San Antonio rolled 20–3.

1958: San Antonio catcher Jesse Gonder drives in eight runs with two homers and two singles in a 13–2 rout of Houston. Gonder went on to play parts of nine seasons in the Major Leagues.

1963: Camilo Estevis strikes out fourteen Tulsa batters and leads Albuquerque to a 5–1 victory. The victory was his twelfth complete game of the season; he would finish the season with a league-high nineteen.

1995: Wichita scores fourteen runs in the second inning of a 22–10 thrashing of Arkansas. The Wranglers scored thirteen of those runs after two outs.

JULY 31

1889: League president Louis Newberg issues an edict that all umpires are to enforce all the rules to the letter. This came one day after Austin catcher Bert Duane hit umpire G.P. Fritz during an argument and stayed in the game.

1934: After holding Dallas to just two runs and eleven hits in eighteen innings, Houston pitcher Bill Beckman scores the winning run in the home half of the eighteenth for a 3–2 victory. Beckman punched a one-out single, his second hit of the game, and then scored moments later when center fielder Lynn King tripled down the left-field line. Joe Vance, the hard-luck loser for Dallas, also pitched all eighteen innings.

1951: Beaumont's Tom Gorman ends a stretch of forty-two consecutive scoreless innings when he gives up two runs in the eighth inning of a 2–0 loss to Tulsa. The streak began July 14 with eight shutout innings in a 3–2 win over Oklahoma City. On July 17, Gorman threw a 6–0 shutout against Tulsa, followed by a 7–0 whitewash of Fort Worth on July 22. He

Bill Valentine served as an umpire, broadcaster and team executive in the Texas League. *Texas League collection.*

blanked Fort Worth again on July 26, winning 5–0. Gorman broke the mark of forty-one set by Waco's Harry Guyn in 1907, and no one has matched Gorman since.

1963: Tulsa's Jim Beauchamp hits the first pitch he sees for a game-ending grand slam, leading the Texas League All-Stars to a 7–3 win over the Houston Colt .45s. Houston's Dick Drott had walked the bases full before Beauchamp hit his two-out game-ender in front of 8,816 fans in San Antonio.

1998: A suspicious-looking rental truck parked across the street from Arkansas' Ray Winder Field prompts the police to block off the street, summon the bomb squad and consider evacuating the ballpark. When alerted, General Manager Bill Valentine defused the situation, explaining that the truck was carrying hair-care products to be given away to fans after the game.

2000: El Paso manager Bobby Dickerson puts nine left-handed hitters in the lineup against San Antonio's ace right-hander Luke Prokopec. The Diablos won 7–4, with Alex Cintron going three for five with five RBIs.

August

AUGUST 1

1896: In another odd turn in an odd season, Fort Worth, Paris, Denison and Dallas drop out of the league. Because of assorted franchise moves, the league played three different schedules in 1896, with Fort Worth winning the first, Houston the second and Galveston the third. When Fort Worth folded, Houston and Galveston played a best-of-nine series for the league championship, which Houston took five games to two.

1896: Houston pounds out thirty-three hits in a 27–9 blowout of Austin. Pitcher John Roach and first baseman Charlie Shaffer both had five hits in a game that saw a total of forty-five hits and fourteen errors.

1919: Beaumont's Bill Bailey holds Waco to just three hits in an 18–2 blowout. Bailey, who had given up seventeen hits to Shreveport in a previous outing, wound up leading the league in both strikeouts (277) and walks (185) in 1919, and he also won twenty-four games.

1958: Ike Boone, the last man to hit .400 in the Texas League, dies at the age of sixty-one at his home in Northport, Alabama. Boone hit .402 for San Antonio in 1923. A career .370 hitter in the minors, Boone topped .400 in a single season four times.

1970: Amarillo is forced to postpone a game because of wet grounds in the middle of the summer, as pranksters had turned on the sprinkler system and flooded the field at Potter County Memorial Stadium.

1976: Just 822 fans turn out to see an exhibition game in Corpus Christi between El Paso and the Gulf States League's Corpus Christi Gulls. El Paso won 13–8.

1998: A game in Wichita has to be suspended in the seventh inning after the Wranglers' Carlos Febles dislodges the anchor for second base on a stolen-base attempt. All attempts to repair the damage failed, including an effort to install a home plate at second base.

2009: Midland pitchers Jason Fernandez and Arnold Leon combine on a no-hitter in the second game of a double-header against Corpus Christi, winning 5–0.

AUGUST 2

1895: Six of the nine men in Sherman's lineup collect at least three hits each in a 26–4 rout of Austin that included a thirteen-run fourth inning. Klondike Douglas led Sherman with four hits and scored seven runs for the winners. Douglas was in the Major Leagues the next season, launching a career that included 748 games in nine years.

1919: Beaumont collects twenty hits and clobbers Waco 22–3, thanks mostly to an eleven-run first inning. Leadoff man Goldie Rapp scored six times and stole six bases.

1936: Texas League hitters pound out a total of 120 hits in five games. Galveston had the most, with 16, while both the Tulsa-Galveston and Houston–Oklahoma City games produced 28 hits.

1941: Shreveport pitcher Ralph "Bruz" Hamner racks up a league-record eleven assists.

1947: Fort Worth's Dwain "Lefty" Sloat pitches a masterful 1–0 no-hitter against Tulsa, allowing just three base runners. The Cats scored the game's only run on back-to-back doubles by Dave Pluss and Monty Basgall in the eighth inning. Sloat won seventeen games for Fort Worth in 1947, a career high, and had the league's best ERA at 1.99.

1952: In the first meeting between African American pitchers in league history, Oklahoma City's Bill Greason tops Dave Hoskins and the Dallas Eagles 3–2 in the seven-inning opener of a double-header at Dallas.

1958: San Antonio groundskeeper John Oliveria and umpire Mike Runyon exchange blows at the end of the Missions' 6–5 loss to Houston. San Antonio manager Grady Hatton and police had to separate the combatants.

1965: Amarillo snaps a streak of fifty-eight innings without a run with a second-inning homer by Jim Mahoney. The streak began on July 26 during a 4–3 loss to Dallas–Fort Worth. The Spurs then blanked Amarillo 5–0 and 2–0, Austin swept the Sonics 1–0 and 2–0 and then Tulsa shut them out 8–0.

1976: The Texas Rangers hand the Texas League All-Stars their worst pounding ever in an 18–4 decision in San Antonio.

1977: John Yeglinski, who had hit just one home run in his previous 205 at-bats, hits three in Arkansas' 11–7 victory over El Paso. He finished the season with four, the last four of his career.

AUGUST 3

1897: The league's franchise in Austin folds, and four days later, San Antonio is dropped from the league to even out the schedule. San Antonio actually had a winning record (68-45).

1904: After compiling a 23-69 record, Paris disbands. The franchise was sold to a group in Ardmore that agreed to assume Paris's record and complete the schedule. The team finished 26-75, forty-five games behind pennant-winning Fort Worth.

1930: Dizzy Dean, who had been a successful amateur pitcher in San Antonio when assigned to Fort Sam Houston, beats San Antonio 12–1 in his Texas League debut. Dean struck out fourteen.

Doug Brocail strung together thirty scoreless innings for Wichita in 1991. *Texas League collection.*

1991: Wichita pitcher Doug Brocail begins a string of thirty consecutive scoreless innings, which include three nine-inning, complete-game shutouts. Brocail, the San Diego Padres' first-round draft pick in 1986, played fifteen seasons in the Major Leagues.

AUGUST 4

1902: Paris right fielder Eddie Pleiss becomes the first Texas League player to hit three triples in a game in a 16–5 rout of Fort Worth. He had just two more triples in all of 1902.

1906: William Jack Jarvis of Fort Worth, who had broken in with the Cats in 1895, beats Waco with a no-hitter, 6–0. Jarvis was a sixteen-game winner for Fort Worth in 1906.

1909: Al Klawitter of Shreveport wins both games of a double-header against Galveston, 5–2 and 2–1. Klawitter, just twenty at the time, went on to win 149 games in the minor leagues and appear in 15 games in the Major Leagues.

1937: Five San Antonio players are shaken up when the Rock Island Short Line Flyer en route from Tulsa to Galveston collides with a terminal engine in Houston. Members of the Beaumont club also were on the train, but none were hurt. All the San Antonio players were checked at the hospital when they arrived in Galveston, and there were no major injuries.

1941: Two Oklahoma City pitchers lead the Indians to a double-header sweep of Fort Worth. In the first game, Eddie Marleau pitched 9.2 innings of shutout relief and started a two-run rally in the top of the fifteenth as Oklahoma City won 5–3. In the second game, Stan Goletz allowed seven hits and two runs, and his three-run triple drove in the go-ahead runs in a 5–2 victory.

Tom Walker (right) pitched a fifteen-inning no-hitter for Dallas–Fort Worth in 1971. *Texas League collection.*

1949: San Antonio and Oklahoma City pitchers combine to walk a record twenty-nine men in a 13–13 game called in the eleventh inning because of a curfew.

1959: Tulsa's Willie Garcia walks eleven batters in 8.2 innings and still comes away with a 12–8 victory over the Mexico City Tigers. Four pitchers in the game—including the loser, future big-leaguer Luis Tiant—combined to walk twenty-three batters.

1970: Albuquerque's Larry McDowell throws a no-hitter against Amarillo, winning 12–0 and earning a $250 raise from the Los Angeles Dodgers. McDowell went 10-9 for Albuquerque in 1970, and his career ended in 1972.

1971: Dallas–Fort Worth's Tommy Walker pitches a fifteen-inning no-hitter, beating Albuquerque 1–0. Walker struck out eleven, walked four and faced just two more than the minimum forty-five batters. Enos Cabell ended the marathon with a two-out double to score Mike Reinbach. Spurs manager Cal Ripken Sr. said later he would have replaced Walker if the game had continued past the fifteenth.

2012: Corpus Christi scores eleven runs in the top of the ninth to shock Midland 17–6. Marc Krauss started the inning with a solo homer for the Hooks, and he drove in three more runs his second time to the plate.

AUGUST 5

Gene Rye blasted three homers and drove in eight runs for Waco on August 5, 1930. *Texas League collection.*

1905: In its first day in the league replacing the disbanded team from Paris, Ardmore commits ten errors in a 4–2 loss to Dallas.

1930: Waco's Gene Rye hits three home runs and drives in eight runs in one inning against Beaumont. Rye, a stocky and bowlegged left fielder, led off the eighth with a homer off Jerry Mallet. The second time up, he hit one off Walter Newman. And the last time, he topped the eighteen-run inning with a grand slam as Waco romped 20–7. Coincidentally, the game was the first night game ever broadcast in the Texas League.

1947: Willie Ramsdell, Fort Worth's veteran knuckleballer, beats Tulsa with a four-hit shutout for his thirteenth consecutive victory. Ramsdell would finish the season 21-5.

1967: El Paso pitcher Jorge Rubio staggers to a 5–1 victory over Dallas–Fort Worth, allowing nine hits, walking six, delivering three wild pitches and balking once. He was helped by a triple play in the first inning.

1971: After not hitting a homer in eighty-eight at-bats for Arkansas, Bill Brooks connects for two against Jacksonville. But the leadoff man lost credit for them when the game was washed out by rain before the end of the fifth inning.

1974: A skunk in the outfield causes a series of delays during Victoria's 11–2 victory over Arkansas. It spent most of the last three innings against the outfield wall, occasionally wandering toward one of the outfielders.

1976: Amarillo beats El Paso 7–3 despite getting just two hits, both in the ninth inning. In the first eight innings, El Paso committed six errors and walked nine batters, allowing the Gold Sox to build a 4–3 lead. Chuck Baker broke up the no-hitter with one out in the ninth, leading to three more Amarillo runs and a loss for Balor Moore.

1976: Jackson's Roy Lee Jackson stifles Lafayette 4–0 on a one-hitter in the first game of a double-header, and then Jackson's Mike Rowland follows with a no-hitter in the nightcap. Second baseman Wendell Kim drove in the only run in the game with a fifth-inning single.

1979: San Antonio pitchers strike out sixteen Midland hitters but also give up seventeen hits as the Cubs top the Dodgers 8–2. Carlos Lezcano went four for five with two doubles and a homer for the Cubs.

1981: Dave Dravecky strikes out 13 and does not walk a man in 10 innings but does not get the decision as Amarillo slips past El Paso 3–2 in 11 innings. Dravecky went 15-5 and struck out 141 in 172 innings in 1981; his Major League career was cut short by a battle with cancer in his pitching arm.

1991: San Antonio's Steve Finken goes six for seven in the Missions' 18–6 romp at El Paso. The third baseman led a twenty-five-hit attack that included a ten-run second inning.

1998: Glenn Davis, who had twenty homers at Class-A Vero Beach, rips a home run in his first at-bat in Double-A during a seven-run outburst against Wichita by the San Antonio Missions.

San Antonio's Glenn Davis homered in his first Double-A at-bat. *Photo by Jim Vasaldua.*

AUGUST 6

1915: Houston and Dallas battle fifteen innings to a scoreless tie. Both starters, Skelton L. Napier of Houston and Dallas's Gus Bono, pitched complete games. Bono limited the Buffs to three hits. Napier gave up five hits and struck out seventeen. Napier played eight seasons in the Texas League, winning 109 games. Bono was 64-59 in Texas League contests.

1972: An invasion of grasshoppers causes the postponement of the second game of a double-header in Midland. The contest was suspended in the top of the first when the plague of locusts scattered players and the nine hundred fans in attendance.

1993: Wichita left-hander Nate Cromwell beats San Antonio 1–0 on just three hits—and supplies the game's only run with a homer in the third. The hit was one of three Cromwell had all season.

1996: Jackson's Edgar Ramos throws a no-hitter, beating Shreveport 3–0. Ramos walked four and hit two batters but was aided by two double plays and an errorless defense. The right-hander had just recently been promoted from Class A, where he had been 9-0 with a 1.51 ERA.

2001: In a 6–5 loss to Round Rock, Midland outfielder Jacques Landry steals two bases to become only the fourth player in league history to hit thirty home runs and steal thirty bases in a single season.

THIRTY-THIRTY MEN

Only four players have hit at least thirty home runs and stolen at least thirty bases in league history: Paul Easterling of Beaumont in 1932 (thirty-six homers, thirty stolen bases), Jose Cardenal of El Paso in 1963 (thirty-six and thirty-five), Darryl Strawberry of Jackson in 1982 (thirty-four and forty-five) and Jacques Landry of Midland in 2001 (thirty-six and thirty-seven).

AUGUST 7

1910: Harry Ables of San Antonio strikes out the first ten Dallas batters to face him and fifteen overall in a 4–2 victory.

1918: All three scheduled Texas League games end 1–0, as Dallas beats Waco, San Antonio edges Houston and Fort Worth tops Shreveport in twenty innings.

1933: A fire breaks out under the stands during Galveston's "Appreciation Night" for its players, and impatient fans put it out before the fire department arrives. All the proceeds from the gate went directly to the players, who responded by beating Oklahoma City 11–3.

1937: Houston's Walt Alston executes three sacrifices in a nine-inning game, tying a league record. Alston followed a less-than-stellar playing career with twenty-three seasons as manager of the Brooklyn and then Los Angeles Dodgers, leading Brooklyn to its only World Series title and Los Angeles to three more. He was elected to the National Baseball Hall of Fame in 1983.

1939: Houston pitching allows just two hits in sweeping a double-header from Beaumont. Ted Wilks allowed both of them in the first game, winning 9–0. Frank Barrett delivered a seven-inning no-hitter in the second contest, coming out on top, 1–0. The two-hit double-header is believed to be a league record.

1958: A loose shoelace costs Victoria's Billy Parsons a home run. Parsons led off the fifth by hitting the first pitch out, but umpire Serge Schuster ruled that he had called time at the request of San Antonio outfielder Carlos Castillo, whose shoe had become untied. Parsons went back to the plate and hit a fly ball that was caught for the first out of the inning.

1999: Midland's T.R. Marcinczyk blasts two home runs in an eight-run fifth inning as the RockHounds blast San Antonio 16–1. Marcinczyk, who had a two-run double earlier in the game, led off the fifth with a solo homer and then followed with a three-run blast in his next at-bat.

2000: Mike Zywica ends a brief but productive stay with Tulsa by helping the Drillers to a 13–12 win at Arkansas. Zywica, sent back to Triple-A Oklahoma City after the game, went eight for nineteen with eight RBIs in five games with the Drillers.

AUGUST 8

1910: Galveston's George Hendrichson no-hits Fort Worth, winning 2–0. Hendrichson, who walked three and struck out three, was done in sixty-two minutes.

1951: Omar Tolson finishes off a five-for-five night with a game-winning single in the bottom of the fifteenth as San Antonio tops Oklahoma City 5–4. In two other trips to the plate, Tolson walked.

1959: Victoria's Eddie Rakow starts, pitches every inning and wins both halves of a double-header, beating Veracruz 4–0 on four hits and 7–4 on five hits. Rakow won a combined sixteen games between Double-A and Triple-A in 1959 and had thirteen complete games.

1962: El Paso clubs five home runs in one inning while drubbing Austin 15–4. In the seven-run fifth inning, Charlie Dees, Pete Carmona, Felix Maldonado, Manny Mota and Cap Peterson went deep, tying a modern league record.

1966: Amarillo edges Albuquerque 10–9 despite eight wild pitches, including a league-record six on one inning.

AUGUST 9

1930: Shreveport tops Houston 9–1 in the first Sunday night game in league history.

1947: After thirteen straight victories, Willie Ramsdell of Fort Worth falls to Shreveport 1–0 in 106-degree heat at Shreveport. The knuckleballer went 21-5 for the Cats in 1947 with a 2.25 ERA.

1955: San Antonio left-hander Don Ferrarese begins a record-tying streak of four consecutive shutouts, blanking Tulsa 1–0. He followed with a four-hit, 4–0 whitewash of Oklahoma City on August 14; a six-hit, 7–0 victory over Beaumont on August 18; and a four-hit, 13–0 pounding of Houston on August 24. The four straight shutouts equaled efforts by Houston's Harry Brecheen in 1939 and Tulsa's Jim Blackburn in 1950.

1971: Texas League directors accept Alexandria, Louisiana, as the league's eighth member for the 1972 season. (Exactly one year before, 5,200 fans showed up in Alexandria for a game between Shreveport and Dallas–Fort Worth.)

1978: San Antonio's Mark Nipp loses a perfect game when El Paso's Terry Stupy hits a ball that bounces off Nipp's leg. Third baseman Mike Zouras picked up the ball, but his throw to first was late. Nipp finished with seventeen strikeouts and a one-hitter.

AUGUST 10

1907: San Antonio's Ewing "Buck" Harris throws a no-hitter against Dallas, winning 6–0. Harris was a twenty-three-game winner in 1907, and he won twenty-two more in 1908.

1908: Fort Worth pounds Galveston 25–6, scoring all its runs off Hyder J. Brown. Fort Worth stole sixteen bases and collected twenty-two hits. Brown, the only Galveston pitcher available, walked eight and hit four batters.

1914: After winning fourteen games in a row, pitcher Andy Ware of Houston loses to Beaumont 6–5.

1942: Thirty-seven-year-old Joe Berry pitches Tulsa to a 1–0, no-hit decision over Oklahoma City. The win was one of 248 in the minors for "Jittery Joe."

1955: Dallas second baseman Alex Cosmidis boots an easy ground ball, ending a streak of sixty-two games and 311 chances without a miscue. Dallas went on to beat Beaumont 1–0 in twelve innings, with Red Murff pitching all twelve for Dallas.

1963: Albuquerque and Austin split a double-header, each team winning 1–0. In the first game, Jerry Hummitzsch limited the Dukes to just two hits, and Bill Lucas ended the contest with a two-out home run in the seventh. Camilo Estevis won the nightcap by scattering five hits. Al Norris doubled home the winning run in the top of the seventh.

1980: Midland's Joe Hicks rips three home runs, the final one coming with two outs in the last of the tenth inning, to power the Cubs past Amarillo 13–12. Hicks was four for five with a run-scoring double, two solo homers and a three-run blast.

1998: El Paso's Todd Dunn drives in a career-best nine runs in the Diablos' 11–10 victory over Wichita. In five times to the plate, Dunn doubled, tripled, homered and lofted a sacrifice fly. Dunn hit .313 with twenty-eight doubles in seventy-five games for El Paso in 1998.

AUGUST 11

1910: Rankin "Tex" Johnson of Dallas hurls a 2–0 no-hitter against Galveston. Johnson, who had pitched for Galveston the previous season, singled and scored the first of Dallas's two runs. Johnson went on to pitch parts of three seasons in the big leagues, and his son, Rankin Johnson Jr., appeared in seven games for the Philadelphia A's in 1941.

1922: San Antonio scores nine runs in the bottom of the ninth—after Beaumont had put up seven in the top half—in a wild 18–16 victory. The Bears won on a two-out grand slam by center fielder Moke Meyers.

1930: Shreveport and Houston play the league's first twilight double-header. Shreveport took the first game 7–5, and the second game ended at 8–8 at 10:45 p.m. so that Houston could make its train connection.

1935: Lee Grissom of Fort Worth shuts out Houston twice, 1–0 in nine innings in game one of a double-header and 3–0 in seven innings in game two. Grissom struck out seventeen, walked seven and allowed twelve hits in sixteen innings.

1951: San Antonio's Bob Turley sets a league record with twenty-two strikeouts in a sixteen-inning game against Tulsa that ends at 3–3 because of an 11:30 p.m. curfew. Turley walked seven and gave up twelve hits.

1952: San Antonio's Neill Sheridan hits a long single off the Mission Stadium scoreboard at 2:10 a.m. to bring in Bud Heslet and give the Missions a twenty-inning, 5–4 victory over Oklahoma City.

1954: Calvin Felix's three-run homer in the twelfth inning breaks up a spectacular duel at Fort Worth as the Cats top San Antonio 3–0. Fort Worth's Karl Spooner yielded just two hits and struck out fourteen, and San Antonio's Ryne Duren allowed five hits and fanned fifteen.

1960: San Antonio collects twenty-two hits—twenty of them singles—in an 18–13 victory over Puebla. J.C. Hartman and Paul Popovich each had four singles for the Missions.

San Antonio's Bob Turley set a league record with twenty-two strikeouts against Tulsa in 1951. *Texas League collection.*

1966: Amarillo's Larry Howard hits home runs in his second and third at-bats in the league—after already having homered in his first. Howard had hit .297 with thirteen homers in Class A before his promotion.

1975: Miguel Alvarez, a seventeen-year-old pitcher just promoted to San Antonio from the Gulf Coast League, beats Midland 2–1, holding the Cubs to six hits and two walks. Alvarez's career in baseball lasted just twenty-one games in 1975–76.

1976: San Antonio's Jerry Reed brings a game in El Paso to a temporary halt when a long foul ball in the seventh inning breaks a power line. The damage could not be repaired immediately, so the game was suspended.

1977: Terry Ervin of Jackson is ejected from both games of a double-header against Shreveport despite not playing in either game. The ejections were the result of his comments about balls and strikes from the dugout.

Arkansas' Dallas McPherson drove in eight runs and hit three homers against El Paso in 2003.
Photo by Christie L. Cathey.

1995: Arkansas second baseman Ty Griffin begins a twelve-game hitting streak—and a streak of four games in which he led off each game with a home run. Griffin finished the season with a total of nine homers.

2000: Despite stealing nine bases, El Paso falls to Round Rock 12–3. The Express put up fifteen hits in the contest.

2000: Three Midland batters—Jay Pecci, Mike Lockwood and Cody McKay—each have two hits in a ten-run inning against San Antonio. Twelve straight RockHounds players reached base on nine singles, a double, a walk, a hit batter and a fielders choice as they rolled to a 12–2 victory.

2003: Arkansas' Dallas McPherson hits three homers and drives in eight runs in a 14–4 rout of El Paso. McPherson had been in the league less than two weeks, and he would go on to drive in twenty-seven runs in twenty-eight games in 2003.

AUGUST 12

1916: Waco tops Galveston 4–1 in twenty innings as Waco's Cliff Hill and Galveston's Jim Gudger both pitch complete games. After an error in the top of the twentieth, spitball specialist Gudger gave up three singles and a double to take the loss. Hill went on to win a league-high twenty-three games in 1916, while Gudger won twenty.

1922: Wichita Falls' winning streak ends at twenty-five with a 4–1 loss to Dallas. The streak would be reduced to twenty-four a few days later after league president Doak Roberts forfeited the team's 4–3 win on August 12 against Dallas. Roberts had discovered that Hub Purdue, a veteran pitcher for the Spudders, had jokingly rubbed clear creosote into the seams of the game ball. This caused spitball-throwing Snipe Conley's lips and tongue to become blistered by repeated contact with the tainted ball.

Spitball pitcher Snipe Conley was the victim of a major prank in 1922. *Texas League collection.*

1930: Dizzy Dean strikes out eight, allows seven hits and does not walk a man in his Texas League debut as Houston pounds Fort Worth 14–1. Dean also had a single, a double and a home run in five at-bats.

1950: Fort Worth's Ezra "Pat" McGlothin pitches a no-hitter, defeating Shreveport 2–1. A walk and two errors in the first gave Shreveport its run, but McGlothin did not allow another runner to reach base.

1952: Beaumont's contest with Fort Worth is interrupted by a flock of seagulls landing on the field. After several minutes of harassing the players, the gulls settled into deep center field to watch the game.

1960: Six different Victoria players—including pitcher Jim Raugh, who would toss a complete game—hit home runs in a 10–3 victory at Puebla.

1968: The Texas League All-Stars nip the Houston Astros, beating a member of the Dallas–Fort Worth Spurs, Luis Penalver, who had been called up to the Astros to pitch in the game. Shreveport's Carl Morton, the winning pitcher, drove in Arkansas catcher Sonny Ruberto with the winning run in the twelfth inning.

2001: Jason Lane gets all three Round Rock hits and accounts for all the runs in a 3–0 victory over Wichita. Lane hit a solo homer in the fourth and a two-run shot in the sixth to go with his first-inning single.

AUGUST 13

1904: Corsicana ace Tom Huddleston loses both ends of a double-header to Dallas. In the first game, Curley Maloney, usually the Giants' second baseman, scattered six hits to top Huddleston 6–0. In the second game, Huddleston came on in relief of Luther Burleson and wound up losing 6–5 on a bases-loaded walk in the tenth.

1927: Beaumont outfielder Guy "Rebel" Dunning collapses in the showers following his club's game against Shreveport. Despite first aid and a trip to the hospital, Dunning died the next day. The teams' game scheduled for August 14 was canceled, and all the other games in the league that day were stopped for two minutes of silence in the seventh inning.

1931: Houston wraps up the first in-season playoff series in league history, topping Beaumont 5–2. The Buffs took the best-of-five series three games to one to determine the first-half winner. The unusual series began on July 25 and featured a 4–4 tie in a game called because of darkness, the biggest crowd in the history of Beaumont's Stuart Stadium (more than nine thousand) and a crowd of more than eighteen thousand for the third game in Houston.

1955: In one of the best-pitched double-headers in league history, Oklahoma City's Bartolo DiMaggio throws an eight-inning, 1–0 no-hitter against San Antonio in the first game. In the second, San Antonio's Don Ferrarese struck out eight, including ten in a row, in a 4–0 victory.

1975: Midland tops Shreveport 9–8 to take over first place in the West Division, topping the Cubs' comeback from a thirteen-and-a-half-game deficit at the beginning of August.

2001: Wichita hands Round Rock the third-worst shutout loss in league history, romping 20–0. The only worse beatings were in 1907, when Austin blasted San Antonio 44–0, and two 21–0 beatings in 1974 and 2003.

AUGUST 14

1951: Houston's Wilmer Mizell strikes out the first five Dallas hitters of the game and thirteen of the first eighteen men he faces in a 2–0 victory. "Vinegar Bend" Mizell finished with eighteen strikeouts.

1961: Victoria's Danilo Rivas strikes out eighteen in nine innings of relief—and eventually loses to Tulsa 8–7 in seventeen innings. Rivas entered the game in the ninth inning and did not allow a hit until the sixteenth. Weeks earlier, Rivas lost a ten-inning start in which he struck out eighteen.

1964: San Antonio's Dave Adlesh breaks a league record when he catches his 109th consecutive game for the Bullets. He wound up catching in 138 of the 140 games he played in 1964.

Danilo Rivas struck out eighteen men in a game twice in 1961. *Texas League collection.*

1972: Texas Rangers shortstop Toby Harrah misses the Rangers' game against the Texas League All-Stars in Alexandria, Louisiana. But he has a good reason: he was stricken with appendicitis ninety minutes before game time and had to undergo emergency surgery.

1998: Wichita scores seventeen runs in the final three innings to pound El Paso 23–3. Wranglers outfielder Carlos Beltran led Wichita with five RBIs, and Carlos Febles had four of the team's twenty-two hits. Wichita also benefited from ten walks, including five from Kevin Gallaher, who walked every man he faced in the eighth inning.

2001: Steve Randolph throws the first no-hitter in El Paso Diablos history, beating Arkansas 2–0. Pitchers Nick DeMatteis in 1964 and Felipe Leal in 1967 tossed nine-inning no-hitters for the El Paso Sun Kings.

2004: Nelson Cruz's only hit in nine at-bats—a two-run homer in the twenty-first inning—gives Midland a 7–5 victory over San Antonio in the league's longest game since 1988. The teams played for six hours and forty minutes.

2006: Both Arkansas and Frisco are held to just two hits, but the Travelers come away with a 1–0 victory, thanks to a single, a stolen base, a sacrifice and a groundout in the top of the first inning.

Gene Rye was a power-hitting outfielder for Waco and Houston. *Texas League collection.*

August 15

1915: A hurricane devastates the cities of Galveston and Houston, completely wrecking their ballparks. Houston finished the season, but Galveston disbanded on August 20. Beaumont, Houston and San Antonio players agreed to forgo salary on off days created by the loss of Galveston, thus saving the rest of the schedule.

1932: A hurricane causes $4,000 in damage to Houston's Buff Stadium, stripping the asphalt roofing from the grandstand and ruining much of the outfield fence. Undamaged in the storm were the light towers, which had been built to withstand 120-mile-per-hour winds.

1932: Houston ties a league record with five home runs in the fourth inning of a 15–8 blowout at Tyler. In the nine-run inning, Gene Rye, Bill "Cap" Narleski and Tom Carey led off with consecutive solo homers. Narleski homered again later in the inning. Joe Medwick drove in eight runs in the game with a grand slam, a three-run homer and an RBI double.

1952: Shreveport's Chico Garcia strikes out for the first time in 234 at-bats, a streak dating to July 1. Garcia appeared in just thirty-nine games in the Majors but had a twenty-seven-year career as a player (1944–70) and later served as a manager in Mexico.

1969: Amarillo center fielder Jim Howarth makes a diving catch of Adrian Garrett's two-out, ninth-inning line drive to save Miguel Puente's no-hitter against Shreveport. It was the first no-hitter in Amarillo's history in the league.

1974: Texas Rangers manager Billy Martin inserts himself into the game in the seventh inning of the Rangers' contest with the Texas League All-Stars in Shreveport. Martin, forty-six, committed two errors.

1976: El Paso's Lawrence Rush hits for the cycle, leading his team's 12–3 pounding of Midland. Rush had a two-run triple in the third, a run-scoring single in the sixth, a double in the eighth and a three-run homer in the ninth.

1998: Arkansas scores four runs in the eighth, three in the ninth and one in the tenth to take a 21–20 decision over Jackson. There were forty-nine hits in the game; three players from each club had four hits each. Tyrone Horne ended it in the bottom of the tenth with a solo home run.

El Paso's Lawrence Rush hit for the cycle against Midland in 1976. *Texas League collection.*

2001: Round Rock pitchers combine to strike out seven in a 5–3 loss to Wichita. What made the modest total significant was that it gave the Express one thousand strikeouts for the season—for the second year in a row. The last time a team's pitching staff had one thousand Ks in back-to-back seasons was 1946–47.

August 16

1904: Fort Worth and Corsicana launch a marathon nineteen-game playoff series, which the Oilers ultimately won by taking eleven games, including a forfeit on August 23.

1911: The Austin Senators win their twenty-second straight game, defeating Oklahoma City 8–6.

1957: Tulsa manager Al Widmar is ejected just before the first pitch of a game against Houston after spitting on home plate and kicking dust onto it during the exchange of lineups. Umpire Tex Harper noted, "That's just like walking into a man's office and spitting tobacco juice on his desk. I work at the plate. The plate's my desk."

1959: Tulsa rallies with three runs in the bottom of the eighth to take an 8–5 lead and then pulls off a triple play in the ninth to stop a Corpus Christi rally. With two on and no outs, Giants manager Roy Murray inserted himself as a pinch hitter and lined out to second baseman Jim McKnight. McKnight tossed to first to double off the runner, and a quick relay to second ended the inning.

1963: Rookies Jeff Torborg and Wes Parker each drive in four runs to lead Albuquerque to a 13–8 victory over Austin. Torborg drove in three of his runs with the first home run of his professional career. Parker, a switch hitter, got two RBIs with a home run from the right side and two more from the left side with a single and a triple.

1966: Newly signed Atlanta bonus baby Al Santorini confirms the Braves' judgment by throwing a 2–1 no-hitter in the first game of a double-header with El Paso. The eighteen-year-old, just signed in June, walked four and struck out eight. In forty-eight innings in 1966, he struck out forty-nine hitters.

1971: A crowd of 1,134 shows up at 11:00 a.m. to see Amarillo blank Dallas–Fort Worth 9–0 at Turnpike Stadium in Arlington. The game was a makeup of an earlier rainout that could not be played at night because of a previously scheduled football game.

1973: The Texas League All-Stars and Texas Rangers use orange baseballs for the first three innings of the Rangers' 9–6 victory in Little Rock, Arkansas. When asked their opinion of the ball by the PA announcer, fans respond with resounding boos. Players said the ball was hard to see and harder to grip.

AUGUST 17

1933: Ed Albers, freshly signed off the sandlots of Giddings, Texas, pitches a one-hitter for Beaumont in his Texas League debut. The 1–0 victory was his only win in five appearances in 1933, the second of his three seasons as a pro.

1951: Houston loses its shortstop, Billy Costa, to polio. The thirty-one-year-old infielder had become ill during a train trip to Fort Worth but was able to recover in time for an appearance in the Dixie Series on October 1.

1963: Wade Blasingame goes to a full count to seventeen batters yet still pitches Austin to a 9–2 decision over Albuquerque. Blasingame gave up five hits and walked six.

1973: Thanks to the theft of several cases of baseballs, San Antonio and El Paso used all but four of the balls available in the Dodgers' 10–3 victory at Dudley Field.

1978: Bobby Clark goes five for six with a triple, three home runs and 8 RBIs as El Paso slugs Midland 20–8. It was Clark's second three-homer game of the season. Clark led the league in RBIs (111), home runs (thirty-one) and extra-base hits (seventy-three) in 1978.

2001: Tulsa's Travis Hafner demolishes Round Rock pitching, hitting three home runs and driving in seven runs in an 11–0 victory. Hafner had a three-run blast in the game in the first inning, a solo shot in the fifth and a three-run homer in the sixth.

AUGUST 18

1907: Gene Moore throws a one-hitter in his second start as a professional, giving Dallas a 2–0 victory over Austin. Moore, discovered in the small town of Lancaster, Texas, went on to win 126 games in parts of nine seasons in the league, including 21 for Galveston in 1914. His son, Rowdy Moore, also played for Dallas (1929–30) and was in the Major Leagues for parts of fourteen seasons.

1960: In his debut in a Tulsa uniform, Tommy Hughes stuns Rio Grande Valley by throwing a 1–0 no-hitter. After walking two batters in the first, Hughes retired nineteen in a row before allowing his only other runner, also on a walk. The losing pitcher was future Hall of Famer Gaylord Perry.

1961: Victoria's Wayne Schurr beats San Antonio 1–0, throwing a no-hitter and driving in the game's only run. It was the first no-hit shutout in Victoria's six years in the Texas League.

1961: Tulsa's Harry Fanok throws his league-best eighth shutout of the season as the Oilers top Austin 7–0. Fanok led the league in shutouts and also won sixteen games in 1961, the best season of his career.

1970: Mickey Rivers becomes the first player to hit an inside-the-park grand slam at El Paso's Dudley Field when he delivers in the eighth inning of a 9–5 win over San Antonio. The ball banged off the fence in right field, just out of reach of Marty Miller.

1991: Midland scores nine runs after two outs in the top of the ninth to beat San Antonio 12–3. The Missions wasted a six-hit, eleven-strikeout effort by starter Dennis Cook.

AUGUST 19

1922: Dallas defeats Wichita Falls 4–1, ending the Spudders' twenty-five-game winning streak.

1947: Oklahoma City's Lyman Linde thrills an overflow crowd of 6,812 fans by throwing a 10–0 no-hitter against Shreveport. Linde would go on to win fourteen games for the Indians in 1947.

1962: El Paso first baseman Charlie Dees sets a modern Texas League record, hitting four consecutive home runs to spark an 11–3 rout of Amarillo. Dees hit twenty-three homers for the Sun Kings in 1962 and drove in 118 runs.

1978: Right-hander Juan Arias faces just two over the minimum as he leads Shreveport to a 3–0, no-hit victory over Jackson. Arias finished the 1978 season a combined 11-2 with a 1.62 ERA between Class A and Double-A in his best season in baseball.

1998: After ten scoreless innings in their game at Wichita, the San Antonio Missions score twelve runs in the eleventh inning and go on to win 12–1. The Missions' Angel Pena hit a grand slam and a solo homer in the inning, Mike Metcalfe had a three-run shot, Juan Diaz hit a two-run blast and Glenn Davis added a solo homer. Jack Jones contributed an RBI single. All of the runs were charged to Wichita reliever Steve Prihoda.

2008: Frisco pitchers Neftali Feliz and Trey Hodges combine for a rain-shortened no-hitter as the RoughRiders blank San Antonio 7–0. The game was called with one out in the sixth inning. The twenty-year-old Feliz was 10-6 between Class A and Double-A in 2008 with a 2.69 ERA.

AUGUST 20

1907: Houston tops Austin 1–0 in fifty-seven minutes. Winning pitcher W.E. Hester allowed just two hits, while loser Brooks Gordon gave up three.

1909: Willie Mitchell of San Antonio strikes out twenty Galveston hitters in a nine-inning, 8–0 decision. His record for a nine-inning game would stand until 1978. In his next game, the twenty-year-old left-hander struck out twelve more.

1910: Fort Worth's Bill Lattimore throws a 1–0 no-hitter against Oklahoma City. Within two years, "Slothful Bill" had a new career—as president of the Class-D South Central League.

1929: Charles Stuvengen of Waco hits three homers in consecutive at-bats and drives in seven runs in a 14–10 loss to Dallas. His final homer was a grand slam in the ninth.

1933: Beaumont pitchers walk fifteen while their Oklahoma City counterparts walk ten, setting a league record for bases on balls. Beaumont's second pitcher, Rudy York, walked ten and hit a batter in 5.1 innings but went on to play 1,603 games in the Major Leagues—as a position player.

1974: Tony Pepper's homer in the top of the 15th gives Amarillo a 4–3 victory at Midland in a duel between relief aces. Dave Heaverlo shut out Midland for 7.1 innings. Midland's Bruce Sutter, who entered the game in the 3rd inning, pitched shutout ball for 8.2 innings.

AUGUST 21

1908: Dick "Slats" Slater pitches the Galveston Sandcrabs to a 1–0 no-hit win over the visiting Austin Senators. Galveston scored the only run of the game in the first inning without a hit. Gus Eppler reached on an error, went to second on a wild pitch, stole third and then scored when the throw to third was wild.

1909: More than 1,500 fans travel from Houston to San Antonio to see Houston clinch the pennant. It is believed to be the largest crowd to travel as large a distance to see a baseball game, except for the World Series.

1920: Wichita Falls' Jimmy Zinn pitches a no-hitter in the first game of a double-header against Houston but has to settle for a three-hit victory in the nightcap. Zinn, who went on to win 18 games for the Spudders in 1920, played professionally from 1915 to 1939, including parts of five seasons in the Major Leagues. He won 295 games in the minors and also hit .301.

1924: Shreveport catcher Chuck Rowland throws out five San Antonio Bears base runners trying to steal. Rowland, who was with the Philadelphia A's at the end of the 1923 season, hit .311 for Shreveport in 1924.

1934: In the first game of a double-header, Tulsa first baseman Alex Hooks collects three triples and drives in six runs, leading his club to an 11–7 victory over San Antonio. A dust storm stopped the second game in the fourth inning.

1946: Shreveport's Clarence Gann's streak of 37.1 scoreless innings ends when he is knocked out of the box.

1950: Four members of the Fort Worth Cats are married at home plate at LaGrave Field in front of 9,817 fans. Floral decorations costing $980 surrounded the altar.

1972: Norm Sherry, the forty-one-year-old manager of the Shreveport Captains, catches his first game in five years. Sherry, a former Major Leaguer, was pressed into action when his regular catcher, Larry Hansen, was scratched due to an infected finger.

2000: Midland's Jason Hart hits for the cycle in the RockHounds' final home game of the season. Hart went four for five in the 10–3 victory over Shreveport and completed the cycle with a triple in the eighth.

AUGUST 22

1906: After topping Waco 3–1 in the first game of a double-header at Cleburne, Rick Adams throws a no-hitter in the second game. In eighteen innings, Adams allowed four hits, all in game one, and four walks, all in game two. Adams won twenty-five games for Cleburne, including seven shutouts.

1927: Wichita Falls' Tom Jenkins records three triples in a game against the Dallas Steers. In his five-year Texas League career, Jenkins hit .346 in 564 games.

1938: Tulsa, with twenty-one, and San Antonio, with eighteen, set a league record for assists in a game.

1949: Oklahoma City leaves twenty runners on base and Shreveport strands twelve, setting a league record for two teams. Shreveport wins 10–3 despite issuing fourteen walks and giving up eleven hits.

1954: Fort Worth's Karl Spooner runs his league-leading strikeout total to 242 when he strikes out 15 Tulsa batters on the way to a 2–1 victory. Spooner tied for the league lead in victories with twenty-one and was the runaway winner of the strikeout title with 262.

1963: El Paso leadoff man Julio Linares knocks in five runs with a single and a pair of home runs in the Sun Kings' 12–9 loss to San Antonio. Linares hit .304 for El Paso in 1963 with 102 singles in 153 hits.

1966: Albuquerque's Willie Crawford has a career night in an 11–1 romp over Dallas–Fort Worth, going four for five with a double, a triple, two home runs and eight RBIs. Crawford wound up playing in 1,210 big-league games in parts of fourteen seasons from 1964 to 1977.

1980: Fernando Valenzuela strikes out 15 Amarillo batters in a 3–0 San Antonio victory. The nineteen-year-old Mexican left-hander allowed just two hits as part of a second half that saw him lead the Dodgers to the playoffs and strike out 162 in 174 innings.

AUGUST 23

1925: San Antonio scores ten runs in the ninth inning before recording an out and rallies to beat Waco 12–10. San Antonio's Danny Clark had two hits in the inning, the second one a grand slam. Clark went on to win the batting title at .399.

1971: More than two thousand Amarillo fans down a ton of barbecued beef, compliments of the Texas Cattle Feeders Association, as they watch the Giants beat Dallas–Fort Worth 7–2.

1973: Ron Dunn, hitless in five previous trips to the plate, clubs a two-out homer in the top of the sixteenth to give Midland a 3–2 victory over San Antonio.

1985: El Paso's Jesus Alfaro breaks out of a one-for-twenty-four road slump by going five for five in an 11–2 romp over Midland at home. Alfaro would go four for six the following day, on his way to a .299 average with 112 RBIs.

AUGUST 24

1907: San Antonio wins despite five errors by pitcher Fred (Winchell) Cook.

1920: San Antonio catcher Elmer Johnson and umpire Ed Doyle get into a fistfight during the ninth inning of a game at Beaumont. After the battle, the Bears refused to return to the field despite holding a 3–2 lead, so Doyle forfeited the game to Beaumont.

1924: Clarence "Big Boy" Kraft breaks the minor-league record for home runs with his fiftieth of the season as Fort Worth whips Shreveport 10–3. Kraft would end the season with fifty-five homers, twenty better than the previous league record.

Clarence "Big Boy" Kraft was one of the great sluggers in league history. *Texas League collection.*

1930: Fort Worth's Lil Stoner tops Houston's Tony Kaufman 3–1 in fourteen innings. Both pitchers threw shutout ball for thirteen innings, but Kaufman cracked in the fourteenth, giving up three runs on four hits. Stoner allowed just four hits in the game, two of those coming in the fourteenth.

1940: Fort Worth pitcher Earl Caldwell's string of shutout innings ends at forty. Caldwell wound up playing well into the 1950s and won 139 games in the Texas League.

1955: Dallas's Red Murff wins his twenty-seventh game of the season, beating Oklahoma City 7–1. Just three Texas League pitchers have won twenty or more games in a season since. Murff went on to a long career as a scout; his most notable signing was Nolan Ryan.

1987: When El Paso employees forget to play the national anthem prior to the game, Midland players line up in front of their dugout and produce an a capella version of "The Star-Spangled Banner." Appreciative Diablos fans rewarded the Angels with a round of applause.

2005: Kendrys Morales goes five for five with six RBIs and Erick Aybar is five for six in Arkansas' 15–7 pounding of Wichita. In seventy-four games in 2005, Morales blasted seventeen homers and drove in fifty-four runs while hitting .306. Aybar hit .303 and stole forty-nine bases.

THE HONORED TEN

The following ten Texas League players were named as Minor League Players of the Year on a list compiled by *Baseball America* magazine and the *Sporting News*:

Clarence "Big Boy" Kraft, 1924: Fort Worth's first baseman topped a fifteen-year career by hitting .349 with fifty-five home runs and a league-record 196 RBIs.

Dizzy Dean, 1931: The Houston right-hander led the league in victories (twenty-six) and strikeouts (303) and was second in ERA (1.57).

Howie Pollet, 1941: The nineteen-year-old left-hander went 20-3 with a league-leading 1.16 ERA and 151 strikeouts for Houston. He finished the season with the St. Louis Cardinals, going 5-2 with a 1.93 ERA.

Frank Howard, 1959: The twenty-two-year-old outfielder hit a combined .336 with forty-three homers and 126 RBIs for Victoria and Triple-A Spokane.

Ken Landreaux, 1977: A year after starring at Arizona State, Landreaux hit a combined .357 with twenty-seven home runs and 116 RBIs for El Paso and Triple-A Salt Lake City.

Gregg Jefferies, 1987: Jefferies batted .367 as a nineteen-year-old and had twenty home runs, 101 runs batted in, forty-eight doubles, twenty-six stolen bases and an OPS (on-base plus slugging) of 1.021.

Rick Ankiel, 1999: The left-handed pitcher went a combined 13-3 with a 2.36 ERA and 194 strikeouts for Arkansas and Triple-A Memphis.

Jeff Francis, 2004: Francis was 13-1 in seventeen starts with Tulsa. He had an ERA of 1.98 in 113.2 innings, allowing seventy-three hits and twenty-two walks. He also struck out 147.

Alex Gordon, 2006: Wichita's third baseman had sixty-nine extra-base hits in his first minor-league season. Overall, he hit .325, drove in 101 runs, scored 111 times and stole twenty-two bases.

Mike Trout, 2011: The Arkansas outfielder hit .326 in ninety-one games for the Travelers, driving in thirty-eight runs with eleven home runs, thirteen triples and eighteen doubles. He also stole thirty-three bases.

AUGUST 25

1956: Shreveport's Ken Guettler hits his sixtieth home run of the season during a game with Fort Worth, becoming only the ninth player in baseball history to reach sixty and the first and only in Texas League history.

1960: Fred Whitfield of Tulsa goes eight for ten in a double-header sweep of Victoria. Whitfield hit .310 for the Oilers in 1960, and he wound up playing in 817 games in the Major Leagues from 1962 to 1970.

1966: The name of Arkansas' Travelers Field is changed to Ray Winder Field to honor the longtime Little Rock baseball executive.

1971: Memphis's Scott Northey reaches base seven times on four singles and three walks in a thirteen-inning, 4–3 victory over Birmingham. Northey, son of former big-league outfielder Ron Northey, also stole four bases and scored twice.

San Antonio's Kyle Blanks drove in 107 runs in 2008. *Photo by Christine L. Cathey.*

1987: Greg Harris pitches a nine-inning no-hitter, leading the Wichita Pilots over Midland 7–0. Right fielder Chris Knabenshue's heads-up play saves the no-hitter, as he was able to force John Hotchkiss at second after trapping a line drive off the bat of Duey Davis.

1993: Wichita outfielder Tracy Sanders wraps a two-game run that sees him go nine for eleven with two doubles, three homers and eight RBIs against Midland. Sanders hit .323 in seventy-seven games for the Wranglers in 1993.

2008: San Antonio's Kyle Blanks goes five for six and drives in a career-best 9 runs as the Missions blast Corpus Christi 21–3. Blanks was near the end of a season that saw him drive in a career-best 107 runs.

AUGUST 26

1888: Galveston pounds New Orleans 12–3 and then folds, finishing the season 39-46.

1908: Despite setting a league record by hitting four batters, Dallas pitcher Cliff Bayless pitches a no-hitter against Shreveport, winning 1–0. From all available records, Bayless appeared in just six games in his entire baseball career, going 2-2 for the Dallas Giants in 1908.

1913: Future Hall of Famer Ross Youngs makes his professional debut, playing second base for San Antonio. The appearance was a reward for the sixteen-year-old, who had been shagging practice fly balls all season for the club.

1922: Houston outfielder-manager George Whiteman set a Texas League record by accepting thirteen chances—all handled flawlessly—at third base. The thirty-nine-year-old Whiteman had been in the league on and off since 1905 and would play in the minors until 1929.

1997: Needing to win four of five games at El Paso to win the second half, San Antonio rallies in game one to win 5–4 in ten innings. The Missions triumph the next two days and then rally in the eighth on Keith Johnson's three-run homer and again in the ninth on his two-run triple to knock off the Diablos 9–7 in game four of the series.

Future Hall of Famer Ross Youngs made his pro debut in 1913 at the age of sixteen, appearing in one game for San Antonio. *Photo Courtesy Bain News Service Archives, Library of Congress.*

AUGUST 27

1964: Austin's Julius "Swampfire" Grant picks up a 1–0 win over Fort Worth in just his second Texas League game. Grant, the brother of Major League pitcher Jim "Mudcat" Grant, had been obtained from Monterrey of the Mexican League, where he had been 13-5.

1968: El Paso clinches the West Division despite having its game with Amarillo called in the eleventh inning with the score at 4–4. The Sun Kings got help from San Antonio, which beat Albuquerque.

1975: Umpire Marty Imwalle forfeits the second game of a double-header between Alexandria and Arkansas to the Travelers after a protracted argument with Aces manager Pat Corrales. Corrales wound up with a three-day suspension from the league.

1987: Mike Remlinger, the San Francisco Giants' first-round pick in the June draft, strikes out nine Tulsa batters to open the game and does not allow a hit in seven innings. Shreveport won the game 3–1, and Remlinger went on to play fourteen seasons in the Majors, making the All-Star Game in 2002.

1989: In the last game of the season, El Paso's Greg Edge plays all nine positions in the Diablos' 4–1 victory over Wichita. Edge is charged with the Wranglers' only run, as the only batter he faces from the mound reaches base and scores.

1998: Arkansas' Jose Jimenez clinches the league's ERA title with a 6–0 no-hitter against Shreveport. After losing his only start in the East Division playoffs, Jimenez would go to St. Louis and post a 3-0 record in September.

AUGUST 28

1907: Fort Worth scores five runs in one inning against Temple on one hit and a walk. Temple committed five errors and also had a passed ball.

1929: Wichita Falls' Larry Bettencourt, an All-American football performer for St. Mary's just two years before, hits three home runs in an 8–6 win at San Antonio. His final homer, a two-run blast in the tenth, provided the go-ahead runs.

1952: Fort Worth honors Dallas pitcher Dave Hoskins, the league's first black player, with "Dave Hoskins Night" at LaGrave Field. Hoskins thanked the crowd by beating the Cats 2–0 in the first game of a double-header, winning his twentieth game of the season.

2002: Shreveport batters tie a league record as every one strikes out at least once during the Captains' 3–0 loss to Midland. Rich Harden struck out eleven in seven innings, and Shane Bazzell racked up four more.

AUGUST 29

1922: Shreveport pitcher Jack Slappey, who would go 3-14 in two Texas League seasons, beats Beaumont 7–1 and goes four for four at the plate. Slappey allowed eleven hits and walked five on what was the best day of a pro career that saw him go 34-77 in the minors and 0-1 in three big-league games.

1935: All four Texas League games end in shutouts. At Oklahoma City, San Antonio loses 2–0 in spite of starter Earl Caldwell tossing a two-hitter. At Dallas, Bill Shores beats Fort Worth 7–0 on three hits. At Tulsa, the Oilers are limited to four hits by Beaumont's George Gill, losing 1–0. At Galveston, Max Butcher throws a four-hitter to top Houston 5–0.

1946: Fort Worth's George Pfister sets a league record with four passed balls in a game. The game was an oddity for Pfister, as he was a league defensive leader among catchers.

1959: Tulsa outfielders Jim Beauchamp and Jim Hickman muscle the Oilers to a 15–3 victory over Victoria. Beauchamp hit for the cycle, went five for five and drove in five runs. Hickman added six RBIs.

1974: Amarillo players Dave Heaverlo and Rich Guerra are shot and Guerra's brother is shot and killed in an incident at a San Antonio club. Heaverlo was treated and released from the hospital, while Richard Guerra needed surgery to remove a bullet from his shoulder.

1994: El Paso backup catcher Bob Kappesser plays all nine positions in the Diablos' 7–1 victory at San Antonio. He gave up the Missions' only runs on back-to-back hits in the ninth inning. On the same night, Jeff Barnes of Midland and Matt Witkowski of Wichita also played all nine positions in the Wranglers' 10–6 victory.

2001: The Midland RockHounds fall 8–4 to Arkansas in the last game of a twenty-nine-year run at Midland's Christensen Stadium. Midland's Jay Pecci records the last hit in the park, a single in the bottom of the ninth.

AUGUST 30

1904: Fred Wills of Fort Worth steals three bases in a playoff game against Corsicana. The only other player to steal three in a postseason game was El Paso's Billy Bates, who did it in 1986.

1922: As fans with radio sets tune in for the first time in league history, Fort Worth beats Wichita Falls 6–2. Play-by-play information was fed from the ballpark to the studios of WBAP, where the game was re-created. On September 1, the station began broadcasts from the ballpark.

1925: Houston snaps a seventeen-game losing streak as Frank Barnes tosses a four-hitter to beat Dallas 1–0.

1942: Houston's Paul Dean blanks Tulsa 1–0, allowing the Oilers just two singles. Dean also was credited with the lone RBI in the game, scoring Chester Wieczorek with a groundout.

1949: Despite walking nine, Omar "Turk" Lown of Fort Worth throws a no-hitter against Tulsa, winning 14–0. Lown went 8-1 in twelve appearances for the Cats in 1949 after starting the season 1-7 for Triple-A Montreal.

1954: Fort Worth's Karl Spooner throws thirteen straight balls, filling the bases, to open a game at Oklahoma City—and then goes on to win 2–1 for his twenty-first

Larry "Moose" Stubing was a power-hitting first baseman and a manager in the league. *Texas League collection.*

victory of the season. He also struck out 8, giving him a league-high 260 for the season.

1960: Pepper Thomas drives in the winning runs with a double in the bottom of the ninth as Austin rallies past Tulsa 3–2. The comeback made a winner out of Thomas's roommate, eighteen-year-old Denny Lemaster, who struck out sixteen and finished the season 13-6.

1963: El Paso first baseman Larry Stubing is sidelined for the remainder of the season when he breaks his arm in a fall from a truck. Stubing, who had twenty-seven home runs and thirty-five doubles, was helping a friend move furniture.

1972: Amarillo pitcher Frank Riccelli strikes out 17 in a 4–3 win over San Antonio. Steve Ontiveros brought home the winning run with a single in the bottom of the ninth. Riccelli led the league in strikeouts in 1972 with 183, a career high.

1985: Former Major Leaguer Ken Reitz, winding up his playing career with the Tulsa Drillers, plays all nine positions in the game.

1997: Shreveport pounds out nineteen hits and takes advantage of nine walks to blast Arkansas 23–4 in the season finale. Armando Rios drove in seven runs with two home runs for the Captains.

2001: Wichita's Brandon Berger cracks a fourth-inning home run to become the first Texas League player to reach the forty-homer mark since 1964.

Wichita's Brandon Berger topped forty homers in 2001. *Texas League collection.*

AUGUST 31

1930: Houston hosts the first Texas League night double-header. After Waco edged the Buffs 2–1, Houston took the late game 5–4. The first game was played in just one hour and twenty minutes.

1931: Houston's Dizzy Dean wins his twenty-sixth game of the season, beating Shreveport 7–1. Dean dominated the league in his second season with the Buffs, striking out 303 batters in 304 innings (he and Harry Ables are the only pitchers to top 300 in a Texas League season), winning a league-high twenty-six games and posting a 1.57 ERA, second best in the league.

1932: Dallas's John Whitehead gives up just three hits in each game of a double-header sweep of Tyler. In six seasons in the Texas League, "Silent John" was 63-41.

1950: Wally Post breaks the franchise RBI record, driving in nine runs in Tulsa's 18–2 rout of Shreveport. Post drove in three of those runs with a bases-loaded triple. He also had a two-run homer in the third, a bases-loaded double in the fourth and a one-run single in the eighth.

1950: Fort Worth third baseman Don Hoak hits what looks like a grand slam but gets credit for just a single. With the bases loaded in the sixth against Houston, Hoak smashed a drive over the left-field fence. Fred Strorck, the runner on first, held up to make sure the ball was not caught, and Hoak, running with his head down, passed him. By rule, umpire Bob Smith called Hoak out.

1964: San Antonio clinches first place for the second year in a row—after a fifty-five-year drought—by pounding El Paso 13–6. It was the first back-to-back regular-season titles in the league since Dallas won in 1952–53.

1965: In the second game of a double-header in Austin, umpire Bruce Froemming orders PA announcer Roy Greer from the press box for allegedly "inciting the fans." It was the second incident of the season involving Froemming and the Disch Field press box. On August 4, he threatened to have the press box cleared and the lights turned out.

1975: Midland pounds El Paso 14–5 to clinch its first Texas League division title. The Cubs had overcome a thirteen-and-a-half-game lead by Shreveport.

1977: Despite suffering from a cold, Jackson's Larry Prewitt throws a no-hitter, beating Tulsa 8–1. Prewitt, who had just nine starts in thirty-five appearances for the Mets in 1977, walked two, struck out eight and retired the last seventeen batters he faced.

1990: Wichita shortstop Tim Wallace hits for the cycle in the Wranglers' 9–2 victory over El Paso. Wallace went four for five in recording the first cycle for a Wichita player in Texas League play.

1996: With five players promoted to Triple-A the day before, the San Antonio Missions are forced to let their pitchers hit for themselves. They went two for three in a 5–3 victory in Midland.

1996: Shreveport blasts Arkansas 28–2 on the final day of the regular season. Arkansas used six pitchers, none lasting longer than starter Erik Hiljus's 3.2 innings.

2002: Shreveport bids farewell to the Texas League with a 1–0 victory over Arkansas that takes just ninety-seven minutes. Shreveport had been in the league on and off since 1895 and was 5,124-5,387 in seventy-four seasons.

2003: For the first time in league history, a tiebreaker rule settled a first-place tie in the second half. Wichita swept a double-header from Tulsa on the final day of the season and advanced to the playoffs, thanks to a season-series advantage over the Drillers.

2013: Midland's D'Arby Myers goes hitless in four at-bats, ending his thirty-three-game hitting streak in a 7–1 loss to Frisco. The streak was the longest in professional baseball in 2013.

September

SEPTEMBER 1

Walter "Hickory" Dickson threw shutouts in both ends of a double-header to clinch the pennant for Cleburne in 1906. *Photo Courtesy Bain News Service Archives, Library of Congress.*

1906: Cleburne's Walter "Hickory" Dickson wins his twenty-third and twenty-fourth games of the season by shutting out Fort Worth 2–0 and 2–0 in a season-ending double-header. The sweep clinched the pennant for Cleburne.

1911: Galveston's Grover Brant throws a six-inning no-hitter, beating Houston 3–0 in a game shortened because of darkness. Brant went on to post nine-inning no-hitters for Beaumont in 1912 and 1914.

1923: Galveston's Thomas Connally pitches and wins both ends of a double-header against Shreveport, giving up nine hits in a 2–0 victory and five in a 7–3 decision. Red Ostergard hit a grand slam with one out in the bottom of the seventh and final inning to win the second game. It was the second baseman's sixth home run in the past five days and his fifth grand slam of the season.

1923: Dallas infielder Tom "Blackie" Connolly strikes out, ending a streak of fifty-four games and 176 at-bats without a strikeout. In his five complete seasons in the Texas League, Connolly struck out only seventy-three times, batted over .300 three times and finished with a .308 lifetime average.

1924: Fort Worth claims its fifth straight pennant with a 16–2 rout of Shreveport.

1960: With a two-run homer by Larry Stubing and six-hit pitching by Gaylord Perry, Rio Grande Valley clinches the pennant with a 2–0 victory over Amarillo. Manny Mota, who was on base when Stubing connected, was presented with a watch for scoring the run that clinched the title. Later, Stubing was given a cash award equal to the price of the watch for his homer.

1975: Midland makes the playoffs for the first time after having its game rained out in El Paso.

1977: Tulsa owner Roy Clark makes his Texas League debut as a manager, running the team on Fan Appreciation Night. Clark led the Drillers to a 4–3 victory over Jackson.

2002: San Antonio and Round Rock combine to use a league-record eighteen pitchers in an eighteen-inning game won by the Express, who put up seven runs in the top of the eighteenth inning. The teams also used thirty-eight players, twenty-one by Round Rock, tying league records.

2013: Frisco's Teodoro Martinez goes four for five with a double and two homers, driving in eight runs in a 14–4 rout of Midland.

SEPTEMBER 2

1933: Houston pitcher Bill Beckman singles in the winning run in the bottom of the seventeenth for a 4–3 victory over Beaumont. Beckman, who had three hits, threw all seventeen innings for the Buffs.

1951: Houston and San Antonio set a league record by striking out thirty-one times in a nine-inning game. San Antonio's Bob Turley struck out fourteen and Houston's Wilmer Mizell seventeen in the Buffs' 3–2 victory.

1956: Shreveport's Ken Guettler hits his final home run of the season, his sixty-second, setting a league record that has never been challenged. Guettler had hit forty-one homers in 1955 at Class-B Portsmouth but had never recorded more than thirty in his previous nine seasons in baseball.

1959: Victoria's Carl Warwick claims the league homer title with two in the season finale against Amarillo. The Gold Sox's Al Nagel, meanwhile, went three for six to clinch the batting title and drove in six runs to claim the highest RBI total in the league.

COMEBACK KIDS

Six teams in league history have won playoff championships while having losing records for the season. In 2001, Arkansas beat Northwest Arkansas in the division series and a Round Rock team that had gone 86-54 in the regular season to claim the title after going 66-70. Arkansas also claimed the title in 2008 after going 62-78 in the regular season. Other teams with losing regular-season records that won championships include Corsicana in 1904 (50-51), Austin in 1966 (67-73), Shreveport in 1990 (65-68) and San Antonio in 2002 (68-72).

SEPTEMBER 3

1910: In one of the best-pitched double-headers in league history, San Antonio sweeps Waco, limiting the Navigators to just one hit in fourteen innings and winning twice by the score of 1–0. In the first game, Harry Ables threw a five-strikeout, four-walk, 1–0 no-hitter. In game two, Fritz Blanding held Waco hitless until the fifth, when he gave up an infield hit to center fielder Jimmy Stewart.

1964: Albuquerque's Braxton Bailey drives in six runs with a pair of bases-loaded triples in a 12–9 decision over El Paso.

1977: Tulsa shakes up its lineup for the season finale, with manager Marty Martinez pitching, trainer Danny Wheat leading off and playing playing second base and pitching coach Frank Bolick playing left field and hitting third.

1994: Jackson advances to the league championship series when Tom Nevers and Jeff Ball hit back-to-back home runs with two out in the bottom of the ninth inning of game five of the East Division series against Shreveport.

2004: Round Rock's Luke Scott drives in five runs despite getting just one hit in a 13–6 decision over San Antonio. Scott had a two-run homer, two sacrifice flies and a run-scoring groundout. The next day, Scott hit two home runs and drove in seven runs in a 14–6 victory, and the day after that, he ripped two more homers in a 12–2 decision.

2006: Arkansas beats Springfield 7–3 in the last game at historic Ray Winder Field in Little Rock. The second-largest crowd in Arkansas' one-hundred-year baseball history, 8,307 people showed up for the farewell at the seventy-four-year-old ballpark.

SEPTEMBER 4

1910: Houston and Galveston play three games in one day. After splitting the first two, both of which were five innings, the third was awarded to Houston by forfeit after a third-inning argument. As a result, Dallas won the pennant by one game over the Buffs.

1920: San Antonio wins two games and loses another in a rare triple-header against Beaumont. The first victory came in the resumption of a game incorrectly forfeited to Beaumont by umpire Ben Doyle in the ninth inning on August 24. Beaumont won the first game of the scheduled double-header 8–3, and San Antonio took the finale 3–2.

1963: Tulsa pitcher Tom Hilgendorf, who went into the game with a .098 batting average, drives in four runs with a single and a pair of doubles and beats Amarillo 12–3.

1966: Albuquerque's Bill Larkin claims his twentieth victory of the season, shutting out El Paso 2–0 on a one-hitter. It had been fourteen seasons since the league had a twenty-game winner, and no Texas League pitcher has reached twenty since. Larkin went a combined 4-8 at Albuquerque and Triple-A Spokane in 1967, his last year in professional baseball.

1999: Tulsa clinches the second half of the East Division on the last day of the season, topping Jackson 9–4 in the last game of Jackson's twenty-five-year history in the league.

2010: San Antonio's Matt Clark completes a cycle with a two-run homer in the tenth inning as the Missions top Corpus Christi 7–6.

SEPTEMBER 5

1903: Dallas blanks Waco 5–0 to claim the league's championship playoff series six games to two.

1921: In one of the first known fatal auto accidents among former pro ballplayers, former Texas League player and umpire Bill Sorrells dies in an accident in Fort Worth. He was thirty-eight.

1935: Galveston and Beaumont outfielders are credited with thirty putouts in the Buccaneers' 3–1 victory, a league record.

1936: San Antonio pitcher A.E. "Red" Johnson strikes out five times in a game against Galveston. The effort was not a fluke; Johnson hit .043 while playing for the Missions and the American Association's Milwaukee Brewers in 1936, including going zero for twenty-two against American Association pitching.

1940: Dallas pitcher Ray Starr drives in the go-ahead run in the top of the 21st inning and then completes 12.1 innings of shutout relief in the bottom half as the Rebels beat Oklahoma City 2–1. Starr gave up eight hits and two walks and struck out ten.

1946: Fort Worth uses eight hits, seven walks and seven Tulsa errors to beat the Oilers 11–6. The Cats also turned a triple play in the eighth inning.

1963: San Antonio clinches first place for the first time in fifty-five years by whipping Austin 9–4 in the season finale in front of 2,984 fans.

1966: Managers Hub Kittle of Austin and Vern Rapp of Arkansas are the starting pitchers and utility player Bobby Dews plays all nine positions it the season finale. Austin coach J.W. Porter was the umpire behind the plate in the eighth and ninth innings.

2004: The largest crowd in El Paso's Texas League history, 11,563, shows up for the team's final game in the city. The franchise was purchased by the St. Louis Cardinals and moved to Springfield, Missouri, for the 2005 season.

September 6

1932: Beaumont scores twelve runs, ten of them in a row, in the third inning of a 23–4 romp over Galveston. Hank Greenberg and Frank Reiber singled twice in the inning for the Exporters, who went on to claim the pennant. Nineteen players on Beaumont's roster either had been in the Majors or would go on to play in the big leagues, led by Greenberg, who went on to the National Baseball Hall of Fame.

Hank Greenberg was one of nineteen players on Beaumont's roster in 1932 who would play in the Major Leagues. *Texas League collection.*

1939: Fort Worth's Ray Starr wins both ends of a double-header against Tulsa, 5–3 and 15–2. It was the fifth time "Iron Man" Starr had accomplished the feat. Earlier in 1939, he pitched the last 18.1 innings of a 20-inning Fort Worth victory in which he allowed runs.

1939: Harry "The Cat" Brecheen of the Houston Buffs blanks Beaumont 7–0 for his fourth straight shutout and thirty-eight consecutive shutout inning. Brecheen went on to win 133 games in parts of twelve seasons in the Major Leagues, including a 20-win season in 1948 that also saw him post the National League's best ERA, 2.24.

1940: The day after playing for twenty-one innings and almost four hours the night before, Oklahoma City and Dallas finish in just sixty-one minutes, with the Indians winning 1–0.

1942: Fort Worth makes the playoffs on the strength of Earl Caldwell's no-hitter against Dallas even though the game was called because of rain with no score after five innings. Caldwell, who had broken in with Temple in the short-lived Texas Association in 1926, wound up pitching in the minors until 1954, when he was forty-nine years old. (He went a combined 12-4 for Corpus Christi and Harlingen in the Big State League that season, appearing in thirty-one games.)

SEPTEMBER 7

1913: In the final game of the season, Galveston's C.H. "Jim" Harbin shuts out the San Antonio Bronchos 4–0 in forty-nine minutes, the quickest nine-inning game in league history. Players were encouraged to finish the contest before an approaching storm, as the team did not want to issue rain checks for 1914. The teams combined for twenty hits.

1930: On the final day of the season, Waco manager Del Pratt plays all nine positions, goes four for five at the plate and strikes out a man in his one inning on the mound. The Cubs had twenty hits in the 14–13 victory over Beaumont.

1946: Using the last day of the regular season to rest pitchers and entertain the fans, Tulsa manager Gus Mancuso and Dallas skipper Al Vincent use themselves as their starting pitchers. They both wound up pitching all nine innings, with Tulsa prevailing 11–10.

1950: Beaumont, managed by Rogers Hornsby, clinches the pennant after being nineteen games out in mid-June.

1956: Tulsa's Vicente Amor throws a fourteen-inning, 1–0 shutout against Houston to clinch a spot in the playoffs for the Oilers. Amor, a native of Cuba, scored the go-ahead run in the top of the fourteenth and then retired the Buffs in order in the bottom of the inning.

Tulsa manager Gus Mancuso wrote his own name on the lineup card as the club's pitcher on the final day of the 1946 season. *Texas League collection.*

1956: For the second time in 1956, Austin wins three games in a single day. After beating Dallas 4–3 in twenty innings in a game that ended at 1:05 a.m., the Senators swept the Eagles 7–0 and 9–3. Austin had pulled off the same feat against Oklahoma City on May 30. Despite winning games in bunches, the Senators were unable to claim the pennant.

1958: Austin sweeps a double-header with Victoria on the last day of the season to overtake the idle Dallas Rangers for the final spot in the Texas League playoffs.

1965: Albuquerque's Cleo James is forced to leave a playoff game when he swallows his chewing tobacco. He became dizzy and had to be replaced after one pitch from Tulsa's Frank Montgomery.

1970: Ron Schueler fires a 2–0 no-hitter against San Antonio in what people were thinking would be Shreveport's last game in the league. The Atlanta Braves, who owned the team, moved it to Savannah in the Southern League in 1971. But the Texas League's El Paso franchise was relocated to Louisiana for 1971, preserving baseball in Shreveport.

1970: Albuquerque outlasts El Paso 21–18 in the first game of a double-header, overcoming a 14–4 deficit with a thirteen-run sixth inning. Joe Ferguson had four RBIs in the inning, with a two-run single and a two-run home run. El Paso took the nightcap 7–6 in the last inning on a run-scoring single by forty-seven-year-old manager Del Rice, who went two for three.

1974: Catcher Charlie Berry, who appeared in ninety-nine games for Dallas in 1927, dies in Evanston, Illinois, at the age of sixty-nine. An all-around athlete, Berry went on to play parts of eleven seasons in the Major Leagues and was twice an all-pro selection as an end for Pottsville in the National Football League. After his playing days, he became an umpire and an NFL official. He is the only man to work in an NFL championship game, the College All-Star Game and the World Series in the same year.

PLAYOFF VETERANS

Through the 2013 season, Tulsa owned the league record for the most playoff appearances, with 34, and had the second-most most playoff losses, 110. San Antonio, which is the only remaining city from the league's first season, has the record for the most playoff victories, with 113, and the most losses, 110.

SEPTEMBER 8

1895: Dallas beats Fort Worth 8–5 in the first postseason game in league history. Attendance was reported at "upwards of 2,000 people."

1920: Wichita Falls pitcher Clarence "Rabbit" Darrough delivers a 2–0 no-hit win over league champion Fort Worth in his Texas League debut. Darrough went on to go 61-63 in seven seasons in the minor leagues, including 21-26 with Wichita Falls and Waco in the Texas League.

1921: Galveston shortstop George "Dutch" Distel goes zero for four in stolen-base attempts against San Antonio catcher John Brock.

1948: Mike Garcia closes out his career with Oklahoma City with a one-hit, 1–0 win over Fort Worth, losing a no-hitter with two out in the eighth inning. The "Big Bear" wound up winning 142 games in the big leagues with a career 3.27 ERA, and he twice had the American League's lowest ERA.

1949: Oklahoma City first baseman Herb Conyers clinches the league batting title, hitting .355. It was his fourth batting title in six years in the minors—and his last.

1950: San Antonio uses a double-header sweep of Beaumont—and an unusual triple play—to clinch a spot in the playoffs on the final day of the regular season. In the first game, with two men on base, Missions pitcher Pete Tay fielded a sacrifice bunt by Clint Courtney and fired to third for a force play. Third baseman Charlie Grant relayed to second for another out, and then second baseman Wes Hammer threw to first, where the slow-footed Courtney was called safe. Courtney assumed he was out and went to the dugout—where he was tagged out moments later.

1964: After the Houston Colt .45s announce they are moving the San Antonio club to another city for the 1965 season, National Association of Professional Baseball Leagues president Phil Piton moves the winter baseball meetings, which had been scheduled for San Antonio, to Houston, stating that San Antonio was no longer a minor-league city.

S<small>EPTEMBER</small> 9

1928: In a wild season finale, Waco scores six runs in the top of the ninth—including four on a single—to top Beaumont 9–6. With the bases loaded and two runs in, Jim Battles singled. One runner trotted home, but then Harry Brown, attempting to score from second, barreled into catcher Buzz Phillips. Brown was called safe, but Phillips, taking offense at the collision, attacked him, grabbing him by the neck. As Phillips—who normally was a pitcher—was throttling Brown, two more runners, including Battles, crossed the plate.

Slugger Jerry Witte (fifth from left) hit fifty homers in 1949. *Texas League Collection.*

1949: Dallas's Jerry Witte becomes the second player in league history to hit fifty homers in one season when he hits one on the final day of the season.

1949: Tulsa turns six double plays during a 16–5 pounding of Oklahoma City on the final day of the regular season. Russ Burns crushed two home runs to claim his second straight league RBI title. Both managers also played in the game. Tulsa's Al Vincent caught the final inning protected only by a glove, and Oklahoma City's Joe Vosmik played left field for the last three innings.

1961: Hurricane Carla strikes the Texas coast, forcing the Pan-American Series to be moved from San Antonio and completed at Veracruz. San Antonio took the series in six games, winning three of four played in Veracruz.

2002: Tulsa's Ben Kozlowski and Keith Stamler hold San Antonio without a hit through the first nine innings of the championship series game. Stamler, who relieved Kozlowski in the seventh, gave up a hit in the tenth inning, and the Missions won 1–0.

SEPTEMBER 11

1923: Fort Worth hits into a triple play—for the third time in 1923. The Cats barely noticed, rolling to Texas League and Dixie Series titles.

1925: Charles Miller goes five for five with three home runs and seven RBIs in Dallas's 13–2 romp over Shreveport. Miller blasted a three-run homer in the top of the first, a two-run shot in the fourth and a solo homer in the seventh. Miller also had a run-scoring single in the fifth and a bases-empty single in the ninth.

1932: Houston manager Joe Schultz makes some interesting moves in a double-header against Galveston on the last day of the regular season. Among the oddities in the 6–1 and 6–2 losses was the fact that Schultz used three position players and himself to pitch the first game. He also used his son, Joe Jr., as a pinch hitter, as well as the team's African American mascot/bat boy. Identified in news accounts as "Fritz" and "Snoball," the bat boy likely was the first black player to appear in a Texas League game.

1937: Beaumont's Mark Christman finishes the season with a league-high forty-seven stolen bases in fifty attempts. Christman was promoted to the Detroit Tigers the next season, and oddly, in nine years in the Majors, he stole just seventeen bases in thirty-four attempts.

1937: Galveston's Hank Severeid, forty-six, catches both games of a double-header on the last day of the season. It was his last appearance in a playing career that began in 1908.

1955: Shreveport pitcher Billy Muffett puts the Sports in the league championship series with a 10–0 no-hitter against San Antonio. It was the first no-hitter in Texas League postseason play. Muffett and Shreveport would go on to beat Houston four games to three for the championship.

SEPTEMBER 12

1895: Dallas rallies with seven runs in the eighth and ninth innings and then comes up with two more in the tenth for a 9–7

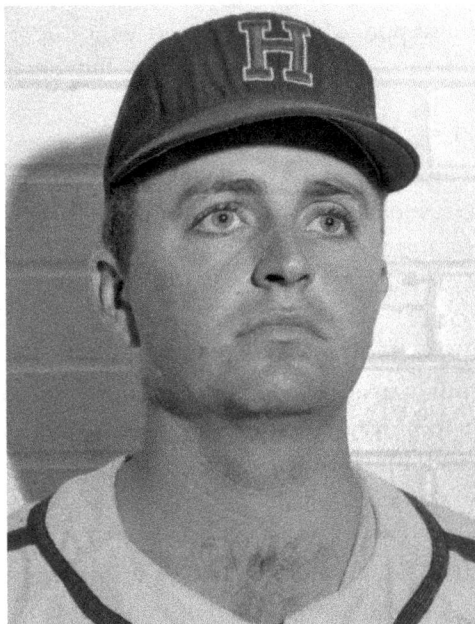

Billy Muffett tossed the first no-hitter in league playoff history in 1955. *Texas League collection.*

Fort Worth's Joe Pate won thirty games twice in the 1920s. *Texas League collection.*

victory over Fort Worth in the first Texas League playoff series.

1896: After losing the first five games of a best-of-fifteen playoff series against Houston, directors of the Galveston club vote to end their participation in the postseason. Galveston won both games on September 12, but Houston got the championship.

1924: Fort Worth left-hander Joe Pate posts his second thirty-win season of the decade, finishing 30-8. He was 30-9 in 1921.

1925: Dallas's Charles "Hack" Miller hits a three-run homer in the first inning, a two-run shot in the fourth and a solo homer in the seventh as part of a five-for-five day and a 13–2 rout of Shreveport. Miller, who played in the minors from 1913 to 1930, was in the middle of a string of six seasons that saw him hit .300 or better, including .329 in 1925.

1935: The Houston Buffs launch a series of postseason exhibition games against the Aztecas club in Mexico City. The Aztecas took the first best-of-seven series 4–2, and the Buffs swept the second 4–0. Grey Clarke went twenty-one for forty-one in the ten games, a .512 average, and starter Joe Sims won three games.

1964: San Antonio teammates Leo Posada and Chuck Harrison hit two home runs each in the deciding game of the Bullets' championship series victory over Tulsa—particularly fitting since Harrison led San Antonio with 119 RBIs during the season and Posada was tied with Joe Morgan for second on the team with 90.

2001: The remaining games of the league championship series are canceled as the result of delays caused by the 9/11 terrorist attacks. Arkansas, which had won both games against Round Rock prior to the attacks, was named league champion.

SO LONG TO DIXIE

The Dixie Series, which matched champions of the Texas League and the Southern Association, began in 1920 when Fort Worth beat Little Rock four games to two. It ended in controversy thirty-eight years later, as segregation laws still in place in the South in the late 1950s forbade African American players from appearing in games, even for visiting teams. Texas League champion Corpus Christi agreed to leave its black players at home for what turned out to be the last Dixie Series. Birmingham won four games to two.

SEPTEMBER 14

1940: A mid-afternoon blaze destroys Dallas's Rebel Field. The fire, which began in the concession stand commissary under the stands behind home plate, threatened homes and businesses around the stadium and took more than one hundred firefighters to put out.

1942: Shreveport's Gordon Maltzberger, a sixteen-game winner during the regular season, records his second shutout in three days in the playoffs against Beaumont. "Maltsy" blanked the Exporters 3–0 on a three-hitter and 4–0 on a two-hitter. The right-hander went on to pitch for the Chicago White Sox from 1943 to 1947.

2011: After more than six hours of baseball, San Antonio pushes across a run in the bottom of the twentieth inning to beat Arkansas 5–4 in the league championship series. The game was the longest postseason contest in league history.

SEPTEMBER 15

1895: Fort Worth's Charlie Meyers hits the first home run in league postseason play, in the eighth game of a series Fort Worth would eventually win 7–6 over Dallas.

1920: Bill Whittaker pitches Fort Worth to a 3–2 victory over Little Rock in the first game of the first Dixie Series, which matched the Texas League champion against the Southern Association champion. "Buzzer" Whittaker went 24-6 for the Panthers in 1920, and he won twenty-three games for Fort Worth the next season.

SEPTEMBER 16

1923: Shreveport tops San Antonio 5–0 on the final day of the season and also wins the postgame skills competition. The Gassers' Ely Shirling was the fastest to circle the bases (14.2 seconds), Smead Jolley had the longest throw (367 feet), Henry Brewer posted the longest hit (433 feet) and John Wight was the fastest in the one-hundred-yard dash (10 seconds).

1959: Austin left-hander Charlie Gorin throws a no-hitter against the Mexico City Reds to clinch the first Pan-American Series. Only an error by third baseman Pepper Thomas prevents a perfect game for Gorin. For his effort, Gorin was presented with a new suit by Austin club president Allen Russell.

2007: San Antonio tops Springfield 11–7 to claim the league championship series and give manager Randy Ready a rare double. Ready was a star in the league in 1982, winning a batting title for El Paso while hitting .375.

Charlie Gorin threw a no-hitter to clinch the Pan-American Series for Austin in 1959. *Texas League collection.*

SEPTEMBER 17

1931: In front of a crowd of 20,074 at Birmingham, the Barons top Houston 1–0 in the opening game of the Dixie Series. The Barons' ace, Ray Caldwell, outpitches Houston's Dizzy Dean, allowing the Buffs just five hits.

2004: Frisco claims its first Texas League championship, rallying to beat Round Rock 6–5 in the fifth game of the seven-game championship series.

SEPTEMBER 20

1895: The first Texas League playoff series, originally scheduled as a best-of-fifteen series, ends when Fort Worth beats Dallas 8–1. The victory gave the Panthers a 7–6 lead in the series, and when Dallas manager Ted Sullivan refused to continue the series the next day, Fort Worth was awarded the championship.

1960: Winning his second start in the series, Tulsa's Dick Hughes outduels Mexico City Tigres rookie Luis Tiant to claim a 3–2 victory and the Pan-Am Series title.

SEPTEMBER 21

1950: Tulsa scores six runs in the top of the eleventh inning on the way to a 13–7 victory at San Antonio. The big hit of the inning was a bases-loaded triple by right fielder Wally Post. The Oilers also benefited from five walks in the inning.

SEPTEMBER 22

1960: Tulsa scores the most runs in league playoff history, beating the Tigres of Mexico City 20–2 in a Pan-American Series game.

SEPTEMBER 24

1924: Fort Worth tops Memphis 14–8 in a Dixie Series game, with the teams combining for thirty-six hits. Ziggy Sears and George Bischoff both went four for four for the Cats, who had twenty-two hits. Sears had hit two homers and driven in four runs the day before in an 11–3 blowout.

1951: In front of 10,711 fans in his home state of Alabama, Houston's Wilmer Mizell strikes out fourteen in a 1–0 Dixie Series victory over Birmingham. Mizell joined the St. Louis Cardinals in 1952 and pitched for nine seasons in the Majors.

September 25

1925: Fort Worth's Joe Pate throws a 1–0 shutout against Atlanta as the Cats win their third consecutive Dixie Series. Pate claimed the deciding game in all three series, and in sixteen Dixie Series starts, he went 10-4. The season also featured Fort Worth's sixth consecutive Texas League title, a record that was never matched.

1926: Dallas scores six runs in the bottom of the ninth to beat New Orleans 7–6 in a Dixie Series game, going on to claim the series four games to two.

1928: Despite walking nine men, Houston's Jim Lindsey gives up just four hits and beats Birmingham 6–4 in game three of the Dixie Series. Lindsey was a twenty-five-game winner for the Buffs in 1928, best in the league.

September 28

1924: Clarence "Big Boy" Kraft of Fort Worth hits three home runs in game four of the Dixie Series against Memphis. The Cats would go on to take the series 4–2. Just two other players in league history have hit three homers in a single playoff game: Springfield's Mark Hamilton in 2007 and Springfield's Chris Swauger in 2012.

1949: Tulsa's Dewey Williams goes three for six and drives in seven runs in a 16–7 Dixie Series victory over Nashville. Williams hit just .271 during the season.

SEPTEMBER 29

1924: Fort Worth and Memphis combine for thirty-six hits in a Dixie Series game. The Cats had twenty-two of them, led by four-for-four days from Ziggy Sears and George Bischoff, and won 14–8. Remarkably, both starting pitchers went the distance. Even more remarkably, the game lasted just two hours and ten minutes. Sears, a .323 hitter during the regular season, had hit two homers the day before.

1928: Frank Barnes pitches 8.2 innings in relief of Jim Lindsey in Houston's 5–1 Dixie Series victory at Birmingham. "Lefty" Barnes, a twenty-game winner during the regular season, entered the game in the first inning with two on and got out of the inning without allowing a run. He shut out the Barons until giving up a solo home run in the ninth.

1939: Fort Worth's Frederick "Firpo" Marberry comes within two outs of a no-hitter in game six of the Dixie Series, giving up a single to Nashville's Woody Williams in the bottom of the ninth. Marberry, who was near the end of a professional career that stretched from 1922 to 1941, finished off the 11–0 victory by getting Calvin Chapman to hit into a game-ending double play.

SEPTEMBER 30

1939: Fort Worth center fielder Walt Cazen wraps up a big Dixie Series against Nashville. In the Cats' seven-game series victory, he drove in sixteen runs and hit .428. Cazen went on to play in the International League for eight seasons, and he is Syracuse's record-holder for career stolen bases and hits in a season.

1950: San Antonio wins its only Dixie Series in seven games over Nashville as Procopio Herrera pitches four perfect innings in relief. The Missions claim the series by taking three of the four games in Nashville.

October

October 3

1932: The Tulsa and Oklahoma City clubs announce they are moving from the Western League to the Texas League.

1991: League president Carl Sawatski dies after a yearlong struggle with leukemia. Sawatski led the Texas League for sixteen seasons, succeeding Bobby Bragan as league leader in December 1975. He played in the Major Leagues for parts of eleven seasons and also served as general manager of the Arkansas Travelers.

Carl Sawatski was president of the league from 1976 to 1991. *Texas League collection.*

OCTOBER 5

1887: The first Texas League organizational meeting is held in Austin. Representatives from Austin, Dallas, Houston, Fort Worth and New Orleans attended.

1977: Ken Guettler, who owns the league record for home runs in a season (sixty-two in 1956), dies suddenly in Jacksonville, Florida. He was fifty. Guettler led the minor leagues in home runs in eight separate seasons.

Ken Guettler still owns the league record for homers in a season with his sixty-two in 1956. *Texas League collection.*

OCTOBER 21

1925: Marvin Goodwin, player-manager of the Houston Buffs, dies from injuries suffered in a plane crash while serving in the Texas National Guard. His death came just weeks after his most successful season as a pitcher (he won twenty games for the Buffs in 1925). Goodwin was one of seventeen pitchers allowed to throw the spitball legally after the pitch was banned in 1920.

November

NOVEMBER 17

1940: John J. McCloskey, who is credited with organizing the Texas League in 1888 and was part of the league's inaugural hall-of-fame class, dies in Louisville, Kentucky, at the age of seventy-eight.

NOVEMBER 25

1929: Texas League president J. Doak Roberts, one of the biggest figures in the early history of the league, dies suddenly in Dallas.

NOVEMBER 28

2008: Red Murff, who in 1955 had one of the single greatest seasons for a pitcher in league history, dies at the age of eighty-seven in Tyler, Texas. In 1955, Murff was 27-11 in forty-three games with a league-best 1.99 ERA. He also led the league with twenty-eight complete games.

December

DECEMBER 8

1958: Tris Speaker, whose Hall of Fame career began with Cleburne in 1906, dies in Lake Whitney, Texas, at the age of seventy. An eighteen-year-old Speaker hit .268 and also pitched for the Railroaders. He went on to hit .345 in twenty-two seasons in the Major Leagues and was the player/manager of the Cleveland Indians when they won the 1920 World Series.

Tris Speaker (right) visits with Brooklyn manager Wilbert Robinson before the 1920 World Series. *Photo Courtesy Bain News Service Archives, Library of Congress.*

DECEMBER 15

1964: Paul Wachtel, who won twenty or more games for Fort Worth in 1919, '20, '21, '22, '24 and '25, dies in San Antonio. He was seventy-six. In addition to his twenty-win seasons for the Cats, he went 19-12 in 1923.

DECEMBER 16

1956: Ziggy Sears, one of the stars of the powerful Fort Worth Cats of the 1920s, dies in Houston at the age of sixty-four. Sears went on to a long career as an umpire, first in the Texas League and then in the Majors. He worked in both the All-Star Game and the World Series. Sears's first partner as a Texas League umpire, Harry Kane, had ejected Sears as a player more often than all the league's other umpires combined.

DECEMBER 26

1948: Left-hander Joe Pate, one of the greatest pitchers in early league history, dies from a heart attack at the age of fifty-six. Pate was the only pitcher in league history to win thirty games in two seasons (1921 and 1924) and went 176-51 for Fort Worth from 1918 to 1925. Pate joined the Philadelphia A's in 1926 and appeared in forty-seven games, going 9-0.

Index

INDEX

Pluss, Dave 155
Pointer, Aaron 122, 141
Pollet, Howie 38, 71, 180
Poloni, John 132
Popovich, Paul 165
Porter, Charles 46
Porter, J.W. 195
Posada, Leo 122, 202
Postema, Pam 66
Post, Wally 188, 205
Potter County Memorial Stadium 154
Pounders, Brooks 107
Power, Ted 51
Powis, Carl 35
Pratt, Andy 23
Pratt, Del 33, 97, 196
Prewitt, Larry 189
Prichard, Bob 35
Prihoda, Steve 175
Prokopec, Luke 152
Puente, Miguel 171
Puffer, Brandon 39
Purdue, Hub 167
Putnam, Ed 36

R

Ragan, Arthur "Rip" 59
Rainey, Bob 118
Rakow, Eddie 162
Rambone, Paul 65
Ramirez, Elvin 52
Ramos, Edgar 160
Ramsdell, Willie 158, 162
Randall, Aaron 36
Randolph, Steve 169
Rapp, Goldie 154
Rapp, Vern 195
Rasmus, Colby 73
Raugh, Jim 167
Raven, Luis 26
Ray Winder Field 59, 152, 181, 193
Ready, Randy 204
Rebel Field 203
Redding, Tim 39
Redford, Fritz 26
Reed, Jerry 165

Register, Steve 75
Reiber, Frank 195
Reilly, Claude 55
Reinbach, Mike 157
Reitz, George 101
Reitz, Ken 187
Remlinger, Mike 184
Renko, Steve 139
Reuss, Jerry 90
Reynolds, Archie 114
Riccelli, Frank 50, 86, 187
Rice, Del 198
Richards, Chris 134
Richards, Jack 149
Richards, Kevin 116
Richardson, Rick 124
Rickey, Branch 127, 148
Riggs, Eric 70
Righetti, Dave 132
Riley, Jim 80
Rio Grande Valley Giants 81, 87
Rios, Armando 187
Ripken, Cal, Sr. 157
Rivas, Danilo 99, 169
Rivers, Mickey 174
Roach, John 153
Roberts, Dave 55, 150
Roberts, Doak 167, 210
Robertson, Daryl 81
Robertson, Jeriome 18
Robinson, Brooks 68, 127
Robinson, Clint 33
Robinson, Don 123
Robinson, Frank 127
Rodebaugh, Ed 103
Rodriguez, Guillermo 115
Rodriguez, Wilfredo 114
Roenicke, Ron 106, 124
Rogers, Brown 119
Rohr, Les 34
Roque, Felix 32
Rorer, Bert 107
Rose, Mike 117
Rosen, Al 34, 109
Rosenthal, Simon "Sy" 36, 112
Ross, David 82
Rowe, Schoolboy 104

Rowland, Chuck 177
Rowland, Mike 159
Rubel, Mike 79
Ruberto, Sonny 167
Rubio, Jorge 158
Rudolph, Ken 38
Rullo, Joe 103
Runyon, Mike 155
Rush, Lawrence 60, 171
Russell, Bill 106
Ruth, Adolph 144
Ryan, Nolan 127, 180
Rye, Gene 22, 158, 170
Ryerson, Greg 61

S

Sample, Billy 35, 81
San Antonio Bears 36, 177
San Antonio Bronchos 20, 196
San Antonio Missions 26, 105, 117, 136, 138, 159, 175, 189
Sanchez, Tino 140
Sanders, James 137
Sanders, Tracy 182
San Diego Padres 16, 74, 149, 156
Santorini, Al 172
Santo, Ron 127
Sasser, Mackey 103
Sawatski, Carl 208
Sax, Dave 23
Sax, Steve 23
Schaeffer, Rudy 138
Scharein, Art 67
Schino, Stanley 135
Schueler, Ron 197
Schultz, Joe 201
Schurr, Wayne 174
Schuster, Jack 139
Schuster, Serge 161
Scott, Luke 193
Scott, Tim 118
Sears, Ziggy 61, 63, 102, 134, 205, 207, 212
Seinsheimer, Joseph 86
Sells, Dave 106

About the Authors

David King

The first ballgame David King ever witnessed was a Texas League contest at Austin's Disch Field in the early 1960s. He went on to write about baseball for three newspapers, and he covered hundreds of Texas League games while working for the *San Antonio Express-News* from 1993 to 2008. He still considers the 1997 season, when the San Antonio Missions ended a thirty-three-year pennant drought, as one of the highlights of his professional career. He is the author or coauthor of seven books, including a 2013 biography of Ross Youngs, the only San Antonio native in the National Baseball Hall of Fame. King lives in New Braunfels, Texas.

Tom Kayser

Tom Kayser has been involved with baseball his entire life. He collected autographs from dozens of Major Leaguers as a child and in his professional career has worked for the Cincinnati Reds and Pittsburgh Pirates, owned and operated a minor-league team and, for the last twenty-two years, served as president of the Texas League. His passion for preserving the league's history is evident in this book, as well as in his previous collaboration with David King, *Baseball in the Lone Star State: The Texas League's Greatest Hits.* Kayser lives in San Antonio, Texas.